ACTIVE RELAXATION:

How to Increase Productivity and Achieve

Balance by Decreasing Stress and Anxiety

Jennifer L. Abel, Ph.D.

D1500902

ISBN: 9 78-0-9827257-0-2

Acknowledgments

I'd like to thank Tom Borkovec for teaching me a wealth of knowledge about anxiety, but mostly for being a great inspiration in the development of my own creative process as a therapist. I'm grateful for Holly Hazlett-Stevens, who made many wonderful suggestions that significantly improved the book. Many thanks to my editor, Katherine Hinkebein, who gave me several useful suggestions, improved the flow of the book, and went beyond the call of duty in guiding me through the challenging process of transforming my manuscript into my first book. I'm grateful for Mary Nienhaus for providing a final copyedit, as well as helpful suggestions that contributed significantly to the book. Thanks to Tino Trovo for Chapter 8, as the seed for these ideas sprouted from his urging me to read Mark Epstein. Many thanks to Dennis Lawler and Jeff Bensky for suggestions on earlier drafts of the opening chapters. This book would not have been possible without my clients. A heartfelt thank-you to them for giving me some of the ideas in this book, but mostly for presenting challenges and inspiration that piqued my creativity. Finally, I'd like to thank my parents, John and Peggy Abel, for supporting my path and teaching me to be independent and resourceful.

Table of Contents

Optional Recordings:

Active and Quiet Relaxation

There are three choices for downloading recordings of relaxation. The six tracks of *active relaxation* that are cited in this book are just $3.99. Should you choose not to purchase these six recordings, there are scripts in the body of the book that you may use instead. There are nine recordings that are for *quiet relaxation* that you may purchase for $4.99. All 15 recordings are available for only $6.99. To purchase these recordings go to my website:
http://www.anxietystlouispsychologist.com
and choose the "Downloads" page or go to:
www.anxietystlouispsychologist.com/Site/downloads.html

Please visit my blog at:
http://balancemeditationstressless.wordpress.com

Chapter 1

An Introduction to Active Relaxation

When most people think of relaxation therapy or relaxation techniques they are likely to think of sitting quietly with their eyes closed. Some think of droning "ohm" repeatedly. Others may think of relaxation as sitting in a hot tub, getting a massage, or systematically tensing and releasing muscles. While all of these traditional forms of relaxation are wonderful ways to relieve stress, they often fall short of making significant changes in the level of stress and anxiety in our daily lives.

The first limitation of traditional relaxation is that it's short-lived. Even those who are able to get deeply relaxed after several minutes of engaging in a relaxation exercise find that the relaxation often disappears completely within the course of a few minutes and seldom lasts more than a couple of hours. The other main problem is that many of the most stressed people actually get more stressed at the thought of closing their eyes and relaxing for several minutes. This is usually due to their drive to succeed and fear of wasting time, but it may also be because they feel too vulnerable.

Active Relaxation solves these issues by providing strategies to directly relax throughout the day. Active Relaxation includes other coping strategies that ultimately decrease anxiety, thereby improving relaxation. In addition, these strategies actually increase productivity, allowing more time for other activities.

The impetus for Active Relaxation came through my work as a clinical psychologist in which I help people overcome anxiety and reduce stress. Over the past twenty years many of the individuals that I have helped to reduce their stress and anxiety are also happy to report that their energy and productivity levels increased. This is a natural byproduct of their stress reduction. They have more time and energy to enjoy leisurely activities, thereby giving them a greater sense of balance and ultimately more happiness.

During the course of one week, two of my clients told me that their workplaces really needed someone like me to help their co-workers accomplish what they themselves had accomplished. One of them marveled at the fact that she had considered herself to be the most stressed in her department of about ten people, but believed she had become the least stressed with the help of the Active Relaxation strategies that are presented in this book. This was the encouragement I needed to start helping people improve their productivity and balance more directly. It was more than ten years ago that I started treating productivity and balance as goals, rather than just as secondary benefits of reducing stress and anxiety.

While many anxiety management specialists work with individuals who have stressful jobs, very few actually have worked in a corporate setting. I have a unique perspective in that I worked in a corporate environment for four years. Therefore, I understand firsthand the many corporate demands and stressors (e.g., demanding supervisors, office politics, difficult clients, and high performance standards). I also have had my own small business for more than twelve years, so I myself face a variety of stressors associated with managing a business (e.g., supervising a billing manager, contesting unfair insurance practices, networking, handling scheduling conflicts, keeping my website current, and dealing with a highly unpredictable ebb and flow of business). I believe that these experiences allow me to be more empathic with people who have stressful jobs and businesses. This gives me a unique and distinctive advantage in assisting and guiding others to more effectively manage stress and anxiety due to work pressures.

While I speak of corporate and business demands, stressors of life do not end there. We all have demands in our personal lives as well. Most of us struggle to find balance among work, family, friends, hobbies, exercise, and relaxation. The more efficient we are in one area, the more time and energy we will have remaining to devote to another area. Finding this balance is a goal of *Active Relaxation*. In recent years, many books have emerged on the subject of happiness, because that is what we all want. You will see that by finding balance you will improve your quality of life and thereby your sense of happiness.

Early in my practice I began to recognize that many people have difficulty learning to relax and thereby miss the opportunity to achieve balance and happiness in their lives. Despite the fact that they were coming to me highly motivated to find relief from various symptoms of stress and anxiety and the concomitant behavioral consequences, too often the old patterns persisted or did not change easily.

As a result, over the past several years I have developed new strategies to accommodate individuals who really want to reduce their symptoms but for one reason or another find that the traditional strategies of relaxation and meditation have left them disappointed and frustrated. These new methods match well with individuals who feel that they can't take the time to do relaxation. Today, I find that I am nearly always able to help people lead a more relaxed, balanced, and productive life, without ever having to close their eyes.

Why do people have a difficult time relaxing? I can think of at least three reasons. One is that they are afraid of "losing their edge." In other words, they are afraid that relaxation will cause them to lose intensity and focus, ultimately resulting in failure. In *Active Relaxation* I will show you that the fear of losing your edge is mythical, at least up to a point. In short, high levels of arousal do not lead to the greatest productivity. In fact, they actually reduce productivity and lead to fatigue, reducing productivity even further. I will show you that by reducing your stress you can become more productive.

A second reason that people have difficulty with relaxation and meditation is an inability to concentrate, or difficulty with concentrating. At least a moderate level of concentration is needed to achieve relaxation. This difficulty or inability to concentrate may be due to a problem with worry, depression, or attention deficit hyperactivity disorder (ADHD). It is paradoxical, but some people with these conditions require more stimulation in order to concentrate on relaxation. With traditional relaxation like diaphragmatic breathing or guided imagery, the mind is so still that there is a lot of competition for unwanted thoughts to creep back in and interfere with relaxation. This is most likely to occur with those who have ADHD. Not only do they get bored easily, but they are also more easily distracted when attempting to engage in the low level of stimulation involved in traditional relaxation. Their minds tend to "trail off" to other things.

The anxious individual often has excessively high levels of mental activity, such that it is very difficult to turn off the worry and concentrate on relaxing. The higher levels of stimulation that occur in *Active Relaxation* are often needed to distract anxious people from their worry. The racing or anxious mind finds deep relaxation impossible when sitting quietly. Much of this problem occurs because the mind is no different from any other natural entity that has momentum; it is not possible to go from "fast" to "stop" immediately. With *Active Relaxation*, the energy of your efforts is closer to the energy of the racing mind than it is with traditional methods of relaxation. You meet the mind where it is and allow a shift of focus rather than trying to "stop it." Rather than sitting aimlessly or running hard, the idea is for the mind to "walk" at a comfortable, yet focused, pace.

The third reason some people are unable to relax is that they were the victims of abuse or otherwise unsafe in the past, or are presently in some kind of danger (e.g., domestic violence). In the latter, worry is adaptive and you should use fear to guide you to safety(e.g., go to a domestic violence shelter), rather than trying to stop worrying. If you were in danger in the past, you had to be on guard in order to shield yourself from harm. You may feel vulnerable, and therefore more anxious, when letting your guard down to engage in traditional relaxation. You currently feel that if you let your guard down, you are risking being harmed. This harm extends to emotional pain that may have occurred in your childhood even if you were never in physical danger.

The habits that were learned in childhood, or perhaps at a later time in your life, were adaptive then, but harmful now. Although you know in your mind that worries are useless, you may still feel that stopping them will leave you vulnerable. You may be so accustomed to keeping your guard up with worrying that you don't realize the extent that it's interfering with your life. Near the conclusion of therapy, many worriers say they didn't realize how bad they felt until they let go of the worries.

With *Active Relaxation*, people actually become more aware of what is going on around them. Therefore, people who have suffered traumatic events should be, and feel, safer than usual. Moreover, they will feel less vulnerable having their eyes open and doing *Active Relaxation* than when their eyes are closed practicing traditional forms of meditation and relaxation. However, if you can't relax because you are afraid of being vulnerable to being harmed, I strongly recommend that you see a therapist who specializes in working with trauma survivors. Even so, this book should be very useful to you as an adjunct to therapy. The skills you will learn are likely to help you feel safer in moving forward, past your trauma.

Active Relaxation begins by providing a rationale for how letting go of stress and anxiety can actually improve your efficiency. The remaining chapters provide strategies that can directly or indirectly improve your productivity level, decrease anxiety, and increase balance and ultimately happiness. That is, some of the strategies are relaxation techniques that directly lead to relaxation. Other techniques are ways to change your behaviors or your thoughts such that relaxation is a result (e.g., time management, changing your thought patterns).

HOW TO USE THIS BOOK

Before getting started, I'd like to provide you with some advice on how to use this book. Think of the strategies provided in Chapters 3 through 16 as tools in a toolbox. Reading a how-to manual, even if well illustrated, is no substitute for actually using these tools. As with many tools, the skill to use them develops over time. Therefore, as you try these tools, don't get discouraged if they don't work the first couple of times you try them. Give them a few days before deciding whether or not they are useful.

Also, do not feel too discouraged if the first couple of strategies aren't very helpful even after practicing them. Some people may find a particular coping strategy to be just short of a miracle, while others might feel that it is useless. Fortunately, those in the second group will find other strategies more helpful. If we think again of a toolbox, some tools may sit in the bottom and you may rarely, if ever, use them. Other moderately useful tools sit in the middle of your toolbox because you use them regularly, but not daily. The most useful tools will sit on top because you will use them daily.

If you simply read this book without trying to apply the suggested coping strategies as you learn them, more than likely they will be of little or no use to you. The strategies will also be of limited use if you try adopting the strategies all at once. To get the best use of this book apply one coping strategy at a time. For example, after reading Chapter 3 wait before moving on to the following chapter. Try the technique of mindfulness for at least a few days, maybe even a week or more, and use the recording [1] that I have included for you in Chapter 3. If you really want to read ahead, that's fine, but try to give each strategy at least a few days' trial before applying the new strategies you read about. After a few days of trying each strategy, you can decide in which tier of the toolbox you would like to keep them.

Most of the tools that are presented will require little or no time for you to put into action. The fact is most people who feel stressed believe they don't have time to

---

[1] *You may purchase the optional recording Active and Quiet Relaxation for just $6.99. I have included scripts so that you may make your own recordings or use them as a guide. The recordings are more involved, but the scripts are ample. There are also several extra recordings of quiet relaxation for which there are no scripts. See page iv for details or go to www.anxietystlouispsychologist.com/Site/ Downloads.html*

manage their stress. If you're concerned that you won't have enough time to apply the strategies, you can put that worry aside. Learning these strategies will actually give you more time eventually. So try to think of the time you put into reading and learning these skills as a good investment: you put in a little time now and eventually you will have more time in return later.

There is a paradox such that those who try too hard to relax add so much pressure that they end up more stressed. Instead of trying really hard, gently apply these strategies. It will be helpful to view your journey to less anxiety and better balance as a process, rather than as an event or goal. For more on the paradox of trying too hard to relax causing more stress, see Chapter 8.

Furthermore, if you are concerned about the costs of letting go of stress, first consider the costs of having it. In 2004, *The New York Times* reported that stress costs over $300 billion to U.S. companies alone. That's more than $7,500 per employee! These costs include decreased productivity, as well as health care costs, missed work, and accidents. In fact, because most occupational accidents are attributed to stress, the Occupational Safety and Health Administration considers stress to be an occupational hazard.

Chapter 2 provides insight into why you have everything to gain and nothing to lose by reducing your stress and anxiety. The remaining chapters help you to achieve stress reduction, thereby increasing productivity, balance, and a greater sense of happiness and well-being.

For your convenience, at the end of each chapter, beginning with the next chapter, is a section called "Live

It," where you will find a summary of how to apply the strategies presented. These summaries will likely prove useful long after you've finished reading the book. I hope you will reflect back on *Active Relaxation* in years to come as being the springboard to your productive, relaxed, and balanced life.

Chapter 2

Afraid of Losing Your Edge?

Everything in moderation, including moderation.
- Mark Twain

Many people live their entire adult lives believing that the higher their stress and arousal levels, the more productive they will be. Do you believe that? Are you afraid that if you relax even a little, your productivity will wane? Perhaps you think something like, "Relaxing might feel good physically and emotionally for a little while, but I really can't afford to relax. If I relax, I'll pay for it later, because I'll have to exert more effort later and I'll risk losing out on being successful."

The belief is that if you want to be successful and achieve, you must be very driven. You might mistakenly believe that the relationship between stress and productivity is a linear one. This incorrect relationship is depicted in Figure 1.

I could write pages and pages about how this attitude toward work, and life in general, is detrimental. And how competitiveness and an excessive drive to succeed in business and make a lot of money are often not worth the sacrifices.

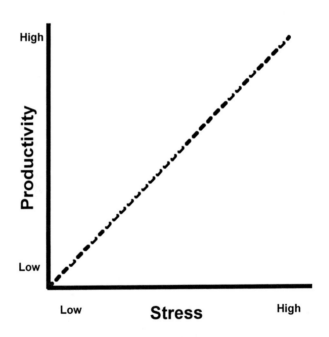

Figure 1. The Myth About the Relationship Between Stress and Productivity

However, I won't do that here as that could be a complete additional book and many people with these attitudes generally do not really want to change. They have little or no interest in balance because their goal is career success at all costs. You are different: Given that you are reading this book, it's clear you do want to change. And even if your primary goal is to become successful in business, you can still achieve more by reducing your stress. That's right! If you carry a lot of stress and anxiety you will find that by systematically reducing your stress, you will enjoy a corresponding increase in productivity, rather than the decrease you may fear.

Whether you are motivated to create balance or be more successful, I have fantastic news for you. It's called the Yerkes-Dodson Law. This law has proven that the relationship between arousal (often experienced as stress and anxiety) and productivity yields a bell-shaped curve such that a moderate level of arousal yields the greatest level of performance or productivity. In other words, increasing your arousal level (energy/alertness) improves your performance up to a point. After this moderate point, higher levels of arousal result in declining performance [Figure 2]. The Yerkes-Dodson Law proved that regardless of what the activity is, if someone is too relaxed (lazy, unmotivated with low arousal), performance will suffer. However, performance suffers every bit as much for someone who is overly stressed.

This makes complete sense if you stop to think about it. When you are most relaxed you are probably on a beach, fishing, lying in bed on a Saturday morning, watching a movie, or the like. You are not productive at

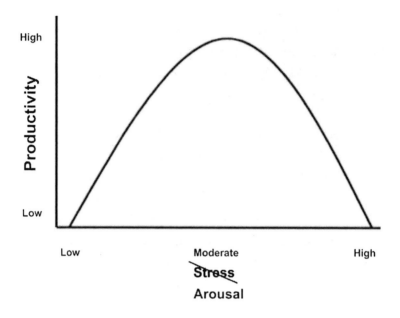

Figure 2. The Yerkes-Dodson Curve

these times (although I will show you later how doing some of these things can ultimately lead to greater productivity).

Now think about when you are really stressed. Your thoughts are racing, unclear, jumbled, and you may find it difficult to concentrate. You may make mistakes, become forgetful, or spend too much time attempting to make something perfect with little return. You might drop something. You could freeze and draw a blank in conversation or thought. You might stutter or slur your words. You might become irritable and difficult to be around such that working with others becomes counterproductive. People will be less likely to help and support you. Loss of sleep is also common and can add to irritability and increased mistakes.

It is also true that a stressed mind tends to be myopic. That is, you see things from only one perspective and your mind is closed to alternative views. Creativity suffers and is frequently even lost. This myopic viewpoint can also interfere in working with others as you may be incapable of seeing their perspective.

Next, consider the effect that stress is having on your body. There is no doubt that this nervous energy will ultimately lead to fatigue, causing - guess what - a decline in productivity! Furthermore stress can also lead to a lower functioning immune system, poor food choices, high blood pressure, as well as hair loss, skin disorders, and gastrointestinal illnesses. If you get sick as a result of this, you once again lose productivity along with time and money going to doctors, buying medicine, and struggling to recuperate.

It is helpful to think about how you actually feel when you are "on a roll." When you are most productive and efficient, you are at a moderate level of arousal. You are alert, motivated, and focused, but not stressed and anxious. If you consider only the aspect of productivity, your goal is to be moderately motivated and challenged rather than highly stressed and anxious.

For a wonderful example of the Yerkes-Dodson Law, reflect on Sarah Hughes at the 2002 Olympics. Sarah, as well as many Americans, had high hopes to win the gold medal in women's figure skating that year. When she went out for her opening skate she was likely too anxious and trying too hard to accomplish a great performance.

Her excessively high arousal level, or nervousness, seemed to result in some mistakes and ultimately resulted in a substandard performance. At the end of the first round she was in fourth place. She was obviously very disappointed, especially after years of rigorous training and the knowledge that she was a favorite for the gold medal.

As you may remember, Sarah's second skate was the performance of a lifetime. Shortly after winning the gold medal, she spoke about what had occurred between the first and second skate. After the first skate she had accepted that she would not be able to earn the gold medal. Given that I was familiar with the Yerkes-Dodson Law, her words were quite memorable. To paraphrase, she said something like this: "I was really nervous during the preliminary skate and afterward I thought I'd blown any opportunity to win the gold medal. Before I went out there again I thought, 'I've waited my whole life for the opportunity to skate in the Olympics and I'm here. I'm not going to get the gold, so I may as well just go out there and enjoy it.' I also thought about my fans who came here to see me skate. Rather than trying to go out there to win a medal, I thought I'd go out there and have fun skating for myself and for the crowd."

What made the difference? Between the first and the second skate she took the edge off with her changed attitude to go out and enjoy the skate. Sarah's thoughts had shifted from trying to skate perfectly and avoid mistakes to a desire to have fun and entertain her fans. This new shift in perspective resulted in a moderate level of arousal that undoubtedly earned her a medal. She skated flawlessly. Sarah and most people who knew her agreed that it was the best skate of her life. The figure skaters who previously stood ahead of her did not perform as well in their second round, and because the second round was worth more points, Sarah won the gold.

Had she skated better in the first round, she probably would have been more anxious in the second round than she was. Even if she had managed to win a medal, it is highly unlikely that she would have skated her personal best. Her mental change of perspective freed her of stress. In upcoming chapters I will discuss how your attitude, or your thoughts, can affect not only your anxiety but also your performance.

We see the Yerkes-Dodson Law in action in baseball as well. Remember Reggie Jackson, Mr. October for the New York Yankees? Hitters like Reggie, who do better when there are men on base or in postseason play, can be a little too relaxed during the year and might benefit from increasing their arousal level. They would probably perform better during the season if there were more on the line. If they created challenges to motivate them and increase their arousal, their performance would likely improve. In contrast, other players hit less well when men are on base and in postseason play. These players may be suffering from performance anxiety. Learning to control that anxiety is likely to help them play better in key situations.

Whether it's athletic performance or performance at a desk job, a creative job, or a job requiring physical labor, the Yerkes-Dodson Law applies. Peak performance occurs at moderate levels of arousal. To enjoy peak performance, moderate levels of stress and anxiety are unnecessary. Rather, a moderate level of arousal can be fueled by positive energy in the form of motivation, challenge, or excitement.

Next let's use the Yerkes-Dodson Curve to do a four-step exercise. Look back at Figure 2 (p. 14) and follow the instructions here. See the example in Figure 3 if you have difficulty understanding the exercise.

1. *Plot a mark on the x-axis (horizontal) indicating what your highest arousal or stress level is on an average day. You can use a SUDS (Subjective Units of Distress Scale) of 0-10 with 0 indicating sleep or as relaxed as you've ever been and 10 indicating a panic attack or most stressed you've ever been.*
2. *On the y-axis (vertical), plot your corresponding productivity level by moving up until you meet the curve and make a mark there.*
3. *Now draw a horizontal line through the Yerkes-Dodson Curve so that you cross the productivity level twice. Find the second spot where the line crosses (to the left) and find the corresponding point on the x-axis.*
4. *Note that the productivity level is the same whether your stress level is very high or very low. Similarly, the productivity level is the same whether your stress level is moderately high or moderately low.*

Now let's take a look at the example of Jill [Figure 3]. Jill considers her highest level of stress for a day to average about an 8. In step 1 she marks her arousal level as such on the x-axis (measure of stress). In step 2 she moves up the y-axis to find her productivity level is between low and moderate when her stress level is that high. For step 3, she draws a horizontal line from that productivity point to find the corresponding spot on the graph where her productivity level is the same. For step 4 she draws a line down to find the point on the x-axis. She finds that her productivity level would be the same if her stress level were a 2 or an 8.

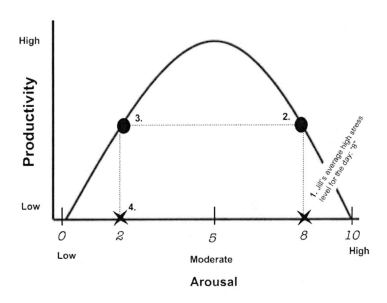

Figure 3. Example of how this exercise would look for Jill.

The primary purpose of this chapter is to dispel the myth that a high level of stress will lead to better performance. You have learned that while arousal is needed to be productive, a moderate level is better than a high level. Moreover, you have discovered that arousal - or energy and motivation to work - can be positive (e.g., excitement, challenge) instead of negative (e.g., tension, anxiety). When you feel stressed at work, remember to try to connect with what you like about your job - the challenging, exciting, or fun part of it. And don't be afraid of losing your edge due to reduced stress and anxiety.

Now that you know you can reduce your stress and still be productive, you are ready to learn how to get into what I call the "peak zone" of the Yerkes-Dodson Law [Figure 4]. The peak zone is the area in which your productivity is high, but your stress or arousal level is

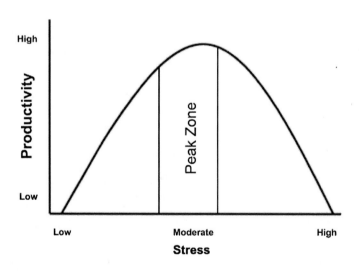

Figure 4. The Peak Zone

moderate. Your goal while working through the remaining chapters is to be in your peak zone.

Note that the peak zone extends further into the low arousal region on the x-axis (horizontal) than to the high region. I included this illustration to depict a couple of conclusions to which I have come. One is that it is worth the feeling of relative relaxation to sacrifice a little bit of productivity. You will be more likely to enjoy your work if you're more relaxed and may find greater motivation to continue. I also believe that if you are reading this book, your productivity will improve even if you find yourself in the lower arousal portion of the peak zone.

The second conclusion I have reached is that if you are in the lower portion of your peak zone, you are conserving energy. This means that you are likely to be able to maintain a productive state for a longer period of time. Also, once you have left work for the day or the weekend, you are likely to more fully enjoy your free time because you will have more energy and will be more relaxed. This is one way in which you can become more balanced. The longer your workday or workweek, the more important it is to aim for the lower portion of the peak zone. This is because you will need to conserve energy in order to sustain productivity later into the day. If you are working for relatively short periods of time, you will want to be at the pinnacle of the peak zone, right at a moderate level of arousal.

Live It!

1. You can lower stress and improve productivity just by remembering that high stress levels are inefficient and that moderate levels (the peak zone) are most efficient.

2. Reconnect with your enthusiasm for your work. Choose motivation, challenge, and excitement over stress and anxiety to get into your peak zone.

CHAPTER 3

MINDFULNESS 101 -
PRESENT MOMENT

Mindfulness is a mental state in which you are aware of thoughts, actions, or motivations. Mindfulness was born out of Buddhism and is an essential factor in the path to enlightenment. However, in recent years it has been used more and more in Western culture as a form of relaxation. [i]

Without always recognizing it, we engage in mindful activities every day. Mindfulness is a very effective way of getting into the peak zone and is a key factor in Active Relaxation.

At this point I hope that you have learned something about the relationship between stress and productivity. You may even be starting to make a paradigm shift

---

[i] *Jon Kabat-Zinn is often credited with bringing mindfulness to Western society. He, along with his colleagues at the Center for Mindfulness at the University of Massachusetts, has proven that mindfulness leads to improvement in a wide variety of performances, from those required of Olympic athletes, to those required in corporate jobs.*

based on a new understanding that very little tension and stress are needed to place you at peak efficiency and productivity. Perhaps you are excited and motivated to start to learn some strategies that will improve your productivity while leaving you feeling less stressed, more balanced, and ultimately happier.

Before I go into detail about the first *Active Relaxation* strategy of mindfulness, I'd like for you to take a moment to consider when you feel most relaxed. Is it when you're watching a movie? Taking a bath? Gardening? Running? Cooking? Once you have decided when you are most reliably relaxed, think about when you are engaged in that activity. Actually take a few seconds to visualize yourself engaged in this activity; put the book down for this exercise.

When you are engaged in this relaxing activity, are you mostly focused in the past, the present, or the future? Before answering this question, you may want to visualize your relaxing activity again. We are most relaxed when we are in the present moment. This is because most of the time there is no threat in the present. All worry and most stress is about the future. Even worry and stress associated with the past or present usually revolves around how it will affect the future. Take the example of a heated argument. It may feel like it is all about the present. However, if you really think about it, what it's really about is what may happen as a result of that argument in the future.

In those very rare moments in which the real threat is actually in the present, we tend to take action. Although we're far from being relaxed, these are the instances in which our stress actually helps us. For example, if a dog runs in front of your car or you hear someone breaking into your residence, the surge of energy in your body helps you to protect yourself and others. Therefore the anxiety you feel is appropriate and welcome.

Now consider when you are most productive at work. Also think about when you are most productive at home. Remember that great feeling of being "on a roll," focused, at peak performance. Again, put the book down for a moment and recall what it feels like to be at peak performance.

Are you primarily in the past? The future? No, once again when you are most productive you are mostly in the present. Productivity does involve some planning and consideration of the future. Certainly, a little bit of reflection is required to learn from past mistakes. However, I believe that almost all tasks require being in the present at least 90 percent of the time in order to be at peak performance.

How can you be in the moment more frequently? By focusing on your senses. Being in the present and being aware of your senses is the essence of mindfulness.

Consider a task that necessitates being productive, involves some level of planning, and is also something that many people enjoy: cooking. Yes, once you have all of the ingredients to start preparing a meal, you do need to consider ahead how much time each dish will require and occasionally look at the clock to consider the timing. You might remember to set a timer as you reflect back on an instance when you burned a dish. However, if you are a productive cook who really enjoys it, most of the time you will be focused on your senses. You will enjoy the smell of the food cooking. You may feel the knife in your hand, the movements involved in chopping, the sound of the knife cutting through a red bell pepper and the chopping sound as it hits the cutting board. You savor the fresh smell of the cut pepper and then you may take a nibble and enjoy the sweet taste, noting the sound and feeling of the crunching in your mouth. At the same time you have remained mindful of the sound and smell of the simmering sauce and the feeling of the heat off the stove. You might feel lettuce or herbs on your fingers as you tear them and smell them. You may also be mindful of the variety of colors and textures you see - the red bell peppers, the green asparagus, the yellow butternut squash, the red meat, the color of the potatoes and the different textures you feel as you hold these foods in your hands.

One could make some similar observations of many experiences, such as fly-fishing, in-line skating, gardening, dancing, making love, or just taking a walk. One of the main reasons people love to do the things that they love is that they feel a mindful connection with these activities. As you think about one of your favorite activities, you will realize that much of your connection to it is the experience of being in the present by focusing on your senses. This mindful focus of the present is a welcome distraction from worries and responsibilities that are weighted heavily in the future.

While leisurely activities are usually the most pleasant way to be in the present, even things on our to-do list can become mindfulness activities. Consider washing the dishes. The next time you wash dishes focus on smelling the soap, feeling the warm water on your

Start Making Scents

Smell reaches the amygdala, the emotional center of the brain, directly. All of the other four senses are first processed in the frontal lobes of the brain that are responsible for higher mental processes. Therefore, smells are much more likely to trigger an emotional response than any of the other senses.

This emotional response makes the senses much more likely to be conditioned to events. For instance, if a woman is raped by a mechanic, the smell of motor oil is more likely to elicit fear and trigger a flashback than seeing him or hearing his voice.

The same is true of pleasant scents as well. That is, smell can have a more immediate and profound relaxing effect. We can even learn to enjoy smells that most others find unpleasant due to conditioning. Rachel Herz is a neuroscientist who loves the smell of skunks. When she was a child she was having a wonderful day with her family when they smelled a skunk. It was a perfect day and everyone in the car was in a good mood and her mother commented that she loved the smell. Because she associated this smell with a very happy day only one time, Rachel now is fond of the smell of skunks.

Take a moment to think about your favorite scent or smell. Perhaps it is something that reminds you of a loved parent, grandparent, or good friend. Maybe it's a scent you associate with a place or a happy time in your life. To help you relax, consider finding an essential oil, incense, or candle that has a similar or the same scent. (This may be more challenging if you like the smell of skunks or moldy basements.) You can purchase essential oils in some health-food stores such as Whole Foods, some vitamin stores, some boutiques, and online. You can burn it in various diffusers around the house or in your office. You can also use an old dishrag, towel, or worn-out piece of clothing. Simply cut or tear a very small piece of the cloth (about two inches square) and put a few drops of oil on it. To protect other things from the oil, wrap a larger piece of dry cloth around it and secure it with a rubber band. The aroma will penetrate through the cloth, but the oil won't. If you can't smell it, you either put too little essential oil on the cloth or you put too much dry cloth around it. You can carry it around and smell it when you're feeling stressed.

hands, seeing the dishes getting clean, and hearing the suds sizzling as the countless tiny bubbles pop. When mowing the lawn, feel the weight of the lawn mower and your grip on the handle, smell the gasoline and the fresh-cut grass, feel the wind and the difference in temperature between the sun and the shade, and observe the green-trimmed freshly cut grass, contrasting it with the appearance of the uncut grass.

Those of you with desk jobs might be thinking that your profession doesn't include that kind of stimulation of all your senses. Maybe your job requires a lot of computer work that limits the engagement of your senses. However, you can focus on what you see, hear, and feel no matter where you are or what you are doing. I am typing now as I am writing this chapter and I am focusing on seeing the words appear on the page, the feeling of my fingers on the keypad, the feeling of my feet on the floor, the sound of my fingers tapping, as well as the sound of cars going by outside my window. This relaxes me and actually helps me to be in the peak zone with my writing. Despite the fact that I am drawing on past experiences, I'm very focused in the moment. I'm typing much more quickly and effectively than if I were to start focusing on the future and how I'll promote the book, how well it will sell, and so forth.

Focusing on your senses helps you to stay in the moment. Being in the moment is useful for relaxing because only rarely is there anything threatening or stressful in a specific moment. It might feel as though there is, but it is really the pressure of the future: fear of losing money, fear of getting fired, desire to make a positive impression for the future, fear of being humiliated, and so on. Furthermore, even thoughts about the past that cause anxiety do so mostly because of the fear about how the past might affect the future.

You can use the accompanying recordings or scripts on the next page to help guide you and train you to be in the moment, thereby becoming mindful. Find at least five minutes each day to engage in a mindful activity. It may be something that you are already doing, or it might be time you carve out of each day. If you already walk, run, garden, or cook you can use these activities for your mindfulness activity. These are just a few examples of activities in which you can practice mindfulness. Alternatively, plan a five-minute walk or take five minutes to sit outside or to look out of a window. You can add aromatherapy, instrumental music, or a nature recording. You can use the optional recordings, use the scripts to make a recording, or use the scripts to help you to be mindful on your own without the recording. However, once you have developed the skill it is best to wean yourself off of the recordings. Nonetheless, during stressful times when your concentration is poor, it is fine to fall back on the recordings. Taking five minutes or more a day will help you to strengthen the skill of relaxing using mindfulness.

Once your mindfulness skill has developed, use it to remain in the moment for most of your day. Become more mindful of beauty on a daily basis. While walking to and from your car or sitting at a stoplight, become more aware of nature. Notice the sky and clouds, the sound of the wind and the birds, the feeling of the sun and the breeze. Also become more aware of the beauty in architecture and other man-made things such as fabric and art. In addition to paying attention to your senses, look for stimulating input into your senses on a regular basis.

Now refer to the audio tracks. When using the audio CD, either leave one ear bud out or turn the volume down so that you can hear sounds in your environment. Below I have listed the preparation for each track as well as scripts that you may use in lieu of the tracks.

TRACK 1 PREPARATION: PUT ON SHOES SUITABLE FOR WALKING AND GO OUTSIDE. IF YOU ARE A RUNNER AND WOULD LIKE TO USE ACTIVE RELAXATION ON YOUR RUN- GO FOR IT! YOU CAN USE THIS MP3 WHILE RUNNING TOO.

> *Begin by focusing on what you see. Noticing the colors, shapes, and textures of plants, buildings, cars. Noticing the trees, seeing the colors and movement of the trees from the wind. Noticing the colors and any movement in the sky: clouds, birds, planes. (pause) As you begin to focus on the horizon, watching how the landscape is changing as you move forward. Feeling your movements, your muscles contracting in your legs, the swinging in your arms. Noticing how the earth below you feels as your feet touch the ground. Feeling the rhythm of your movements. (pause) Noticing the feeling of the breeze. Focusing all of your attention on the breeze, noticing how it feels. Noticing how it moves trees, plants, your hair, the clouds. (pause) Noticing the sound of the breeze in your ear and noticing whether or not you can hear it moving leaves, wind chimes. (pause) Noticing other things that you might hear such as the sound of birds, cars, crickets, dogs. (pause) Noticing if there is something that you smell. (pause) Allowing your mind to float gently between your senses.*

TRACK 2 PREPARATION: RATHER THAN WASHING DISHES NOW, USE THIS RECORDING WHEN YOU WANT TO DO THE DISHES ANYWAY.

As you turn on the water, feeling the knob in your hand and hearing the sound of the water. Watching the water hit the bottom of the sink. Feeling the temperature of the water as you place your hand in the stream and noticing it becoming warmer. Feeling the stopper in your hand and the sound it makes as you insert it. Adding the soap and watching the bubbles forming. (pause) Run a hand through the bubbles, as you begin to smell the soap; inhaling it. (pause) As you place the dishes into the soapy water, feeling each one in your hand and hearing the sound it makes as it goes into the water. Focusing on everything you see, hear, feel, and smell. (pause) Turning off the water and noticing the change in the sound. Grabbing the dishcloth or brush as you feel it in your hand. As you begin to wash the dishes, feeling the movements and pressure as you watch the dish becoming clean.

TRACK 3 PREPARATION: YOU CAN USE THIS TRACK REGARDLESS OF YOUR ACTIVITY. IF YOU CHOOSE YOU CAN USE THIS WHILE SITTING QUIETLY AS WELL.

Begin by noticing the surface or surfaces beneath you. Becoming aware of your arms and legs. Noticing any movement. Feeling your clothing, socks, shoes, and anything else that you may be wearing such as jewelry or glasses. Noticing the sounds that you hear. If it's quiet you can hear the sound of your breathing. Feeling your breathing in your nose and in your lungs. Noticing that the air that you breathe in is cooler, the air that you exhale is warmer. Enjoying the stillness between each breath, right after you breathe out and before you breathe in. Observing what you see. Noticing color, movement, and texture. Seeing shadows, highlights, reflections. Noticing everything that you see, hear, feel, and noticing whether there is anything that you smell.

When you notice yourself beginning to worry or feel stressed, gently shift your attention toward focusing on your senses. As you play the recordings, notice which senses allow you to connect the most with your environment and allow you to relax.

Live It!

1. To live mindfulness strengthen your skill for at least five minutes a day. At first, use the recordings to guide you. Eventually, wean yourself off of the recordings, as research shows people do better with relaxation when it is self-guided. However, you may want to fall back on the recordings as a refresher or at times when you are unable to concentrate.

2. Use mindfulness several times throughout the day. To ensure that you apply it frequently, practice mindfulness without stopping what you are doing. However, when you have the luxury of time or you are feeling particularly stressed, you may choose to take several seconds to a couple of minutes to stop what you're doing to focus exclusively on your senses.

3. In the spirit of Active Relaxation, move and smell the roses. Be more mindful of nature. Notice the sky, the clouds, sunrises and sunsets, flowers, trees, and the sounds of birds and crickets, and observe animals and children.

CHAPTER 4

NIP IT IN THE BUD

An ounce of prevention is worth a pound of cure.
- Benjamin Franklin

A stitch in time saves nine.

Nip it in the bud.

I can think of no other phenomenon that has been expressed using so many different adages. Without a doubt, this is because the utility of early intervention and prevention is undeniable and extensive. It is commonplace to see this fact practiced in medicine. All around us we see examples every day of the importance of early detection. Health insurance companies cover billions of dollars in claims for preventive care, including everything from yearly gynecology visits to colonoscopy screenings to biannual dental visits. These kinds of health screenings, even added up for thousands of insured persons, are much less expensive than treating a handful of cases in which the diseases became much more grave and complex because they weren't detected sooner.

We have all learned that once the disease process has begun, it is much easier to eradicate or control if it is caught early. We could cite hundreds of examples, from cancer to gum disease to multiple sclerosis to something as simple as the common cold. However, we rarely, if ever, hear about catching mental health issues early. Yet it's not at all surprising that catching anxiety and stress early and "nipping it in the bud" is extraordinarily useful.

In fact, if you have a moment and a match, you might try this exercise: Light the match and set fire to a single sheet of paper and blow it out immediately. Now consider how ineffective that blow would be to extinguish the fire just five or ten minutes later, particularly if that piece of paper were near a stack of papers or something equally flammable. Anxiety isn't much different.

Years ago psychologist researchers hypothesized that teaching people to think more positively (cognitive therapy) and using relaxation would be very effective in treating generalized anxiety disorder (i.e., chronic and severe worriers). They were wrong. It wasn't much more helpful than traditional "talk therapy."

However, it was soon realized that anxiety occurs in a spiral of interactions. Worry, in particular, usually starts out mild and progresses insidiously. It may include thoughts, images, physical sensations, behaviors, and emotions that spiral out of control over the course of a few moments (in panic attacks) or over several minutes (worry spirals). It was then realized that the therapeutic methods being taught were not the problem. Instead the real problem was that the potentially helpful techniques were being applied at the wrong time: too late in the spiral. Therefore, it was very likely that the individuals in the aforementioned study waited until the anxiety had gained momentum and had spiraled out of control. Stress and anxiety levels were then too high for the techniques to make a difference.

Once T. D. Borkovec and his group at *Penn State University* taught worriers to catch the onset of their anxiety early and practice cognitive therapy and relaxation frequently throughout the day, the techniques were found to be very effective. In fact, I was a therapist in a study under Tom's direction that compared cognitive therapy, relaxation therapy, and the combination. All groups were taught to catch the anxiety early. My success rate was above 90 percent even with very stringent criteria, and those who didn't succeed would admit that they put little or no effort into it.

Let me give you the following example of an anxiety spiral that I use with my clients. Forgive me for the old-fashioned nature of this example:

Rachel is making dinner and she is very relaxed, into the process of cooking. Then she has a couple of thoughts: "Gee, it seems like it's getting late. I wonder what time it is?" With those thoughts she gets a little tension in the back of her neck. She sets down her knife and walks over to the clock. After looking at the clock Rachel sees that it is, in fact, a little late, which causes the tension in her neck to build and spread down to her back. She automatically walks over to the window, and when she doesn't see her husband's car coming down the road, she immediately gets a knot in her stomach. If it's a beautiful day she might worry that he's having an affair. If it's cloudy or rainy, she concludes that he's been in an accident. She's beyond just being worried now; she is feeling fearful. Soon Rachel has a visual image of her husband's wrecked car and visualizes him in an ambulance, his head bleeding. She hears the sirens in her mind. She begins to pace. Her heart is now racing and pounding with fear. She begins pacing and recalls the times that she has done this in the past and gets really frustrated with him. She thinks, "He knows that I worry about him and yet he does this to me all the time." At that point she is reminded that she has a problem with worry so she tries to think more positively and tries a breathing technique she has learned. This actually makes things a little worse because it uses energy, doesn't help at this stage, and thus causes frustration.

If there were a way for Rachel to recognize the first thought or symptom in the spiral, she could have utilized mindfulness, another relaxation strategy, or cognitive therapy [see Chapters 9 and 10] right away and she would have been fine. She could have let go of the thoughts more easily and prevented the spiral from getting out of control. Unfortunately, most of the time we are not quickly conscious of the fact that we are worried, feeling physically stressed, or frustrated. That awareness only reaches our conscious mind after our anxiety and stress spiral has gathered more momentum, to the point that the strategies are useless.

Whether you have the severe worry and anxiety that Rachel has or whether you're troubled by more moderate stress, it is critical that you catch the spiral before it gets out of control. In other words, regardless of the type and level of your stress there is a two-step process you can take to relieve it. The first step is to become aware of when the spiral starts. The second step is to gently shift to mindfulness or another strategy you've learned in the past or from this book.

Unfortunately, we usually aren't aware of stress and anxiety until there is significant momentum. We also often forget to apply the strategies even after we're aware of our discomfort. Therefore, it is best to find alternatives, namely external reminders, to help us catch the anxiety and nip it in the bud before it gets out of control. Find reminders, things that occur numerous times throughout the day, or create reminders that you will notice multiple times a day. Typically these reminders will be visual and auditory; however, if you have pets or small children, tactile and even olfactory reminders may occur frequently.

For most people, I suggest creating reminders. If you think you would respond best to auditory cues, you can program your computer, phone, or PDA to remind you at some frequent interval, perhaps every fifteen minutes. If you keep your phone or PDA in your pocket, you can switch it to vibrate and have a tactile cue. Once you are accustomed to maintaining relaxation, you can set the reminders less frequently. You can always increase the frequency during times that are more stressful.

For visual cues you can use sticky notes. Put sticky notes in two general places: places you see frequently and places you associate with stress even if it is very infrequently. Rachel, for instance, may check her clock just three or four times weekly, when she thinks her husband is late. But because that can be such a stressful situation for her, the clock is an excellent place for a sticky-note reminder. Other places to put sticky notes include light switches, mirrors, TVs, the refrigerator, the pantry, toilets, a book or magazine that you are reading, and phones. For small items, such as your cell phone, keys, watch, or your remote control, tear off the nonsticky part and attach just the sticky portion to these items.

You might be thinking something like "I don't have time to relax that many times a day. That's why I bought this book." It is imperative that you understand that I am not asking you to stop what you're doing every time you become aware of a reminder. If you do that, you certainly will defeat the purpose of leading a more relaxed lifestyle because the frequent interruptions will become frustrating.

The good news is that you can relax several times daily without stopping. You can be mindful of the moment without ever slowing down! Try it now. Focus your attention on the surfaces beneath you. Notice that you can do that while simultaneously reading without interfering with your speed and comprehension. Likewise, you can engage in any activity without stopping, slowing, or sacrificing quality and still use relaxation and stress reduction strategies, hence the phrase *Active Relaxation*.

In time, the reminders may actually save you time by leading you to be more focused. In the example of Rachel, instead of going to the window and then pacing, she would see her reminder as soon as she looked at the clock. Then she would return to cooking sooner, which would save her time, as the following example illustrates:

Rachel is making dinner and she is very relaxed, into the process of cooking. Then she has a couple of thoughts: "Gee, it seems like it's getting late. I wonder what time it is?" With that thought she gets a little tension in the back of her neck. She sets her knife down and walks over to the clock. She sees the sticky note on the clock and gently shifts her attention to her feet on the floor and the smell of the food. She focuses on the feeling of the knife in her hand and the colors of the cutting board and the veggies she's chopping. She watches the veggies turning into smaller pieces and enjoys a nibble of her favorite vegetable, the red bell pepper. Because she caught her anxiety spiral early and gently applied a coping strategy, within moments she feels as relaxed as she had before she started to wonder about the time.

Rachel's mindfulness strategy is a "no contest" victory over the little bit of tension in her neck and the knowledge that her husband is a little late as usual. Consider the contrast between this scenario and her attempting to use mindfulness against tension in her neck and back, her pounding and racing heart, the knot in her stomach, images of her husband injured, her pacing, her fear, and her frustration.

I expect that you will do these mini-relaxations as many as fifty or more times each day. Actually, many individuals who learn to use reminders as cues indicate that they are letting go of distress several times an hour. Although it is best not to stop that many times a day (i.e., whenever you see or hear one of your reminders), there may be times when you choose to take a few seconds or even a few minutes to practice mindfulness or other strategies (strategies you will learn in upcoming chapters, or those you may know already).

It may be that you already have some very good coping strategies but have found that they are ineffective. If so, consider that perhaps you did not use them until the stress had spiraled too far. If you're like most people, you only tried them after the spiral had gained so much momentum that it was too late in the process for them to be effective. Therefore, I encourage you to again try those strategies that you may have learned and discarded because they were not useful late in the stress spiral. You might be surprised by the results you achieve when you use them early in the spiral.

When you catch your stress spiral early and rapidly, and apply coping strategies at the right time, you accomplish three important things. First, you catch any thoughts, physical sensations, behaviors, emotions, and images while the stress is still weak, such that your coping strategies are strong enough to overpower the anxiety.

Second, you prevent the old spiral from being strengthened in memory. Without realizing it, you have been repeating, practicing, and strengthening your stress spirals, thus making a bad habit stronger and stronger until the spirals became your automatic response. Now, when you catch a spiral early and "nip it in the bud" with your coping strategies, you prevent yourself from practicing it, and this will help you to weaken it. Think of it as putting your stress and anxiety muscles in a sling. With lack of use, the habits begin to weaken and then atrophy.

Finally, each time you catch stress early and apply a coping strategy, you are practicing new behaviors that will become a new habit over time. As soon as you begin to detect stress you automatically release tension, focus on your feet, change your perspective, or employ another coping strategy. This new habit can become so powerful that when I ask individuals what their SUDS (subjective units of distress scale) level is (on a 0 to 10 scale), they ask, "Before or after you asked me?" In other words, just by hearing my question, they automatically apply a stress reduction strategy. After catching anxiety early and applying coping strategies, the new habit of letting go becomes stronger, while the old habit of allowing the stress to build weakens.

When you notice that you are stressed, gently move toward relaxation rather than trying to push the anxiety or frustration away. When you try to push it away you risk adding an element of stress and you focus more on the stress than on the relaxation. To illustrate, imagine thinking "focusing on my senses" versus "push the anxiety away."

> **Sing**
>
> Research shows that singing can relieve stress. It's not clear whether it's because it allows you to express your emotions, lets you shift your attention away from your problems, or because it creates a greater exchange of oxygen and carbon-dioxide. Perhaps it's a combination. So whether you're caught in traffic, in the shower, or somewhere else where it's appropriate, sing!

As you recognize your reminders to use your coping strategies, it is very likely that there will be times when you will think that you're not stressed, and then you may be tempted to not engage in a stress reduction strategy. Do it anyway. Consider that on a 0-10 scale, with 10 being the highest level of stress, your SUDS level is at a 4. This may seem "cool" to you, especially if you tend to hover around a 6 or more. However, might you feel a little bit better and still be every bit as productive at a 3 or even a 2.5? As long as your productivity is not significantly reduced, it's better to be at a lower level of stress.

Most important, if you are at a SUDS level of 4 and something stressful occurs, it might bring you up to a 6 or a 7. If you apply mindfulness at a 4 and you become a 2 or a 3, that same event may not bother you at all or it might only bring you up to a 3 or 4. Remember, an ounce of prevention is worth a pound of cure.

Keep in mind also that after a period of time, you are likely to become desensitized to your reminders. Much like a new piece of art or new furniture, you may notice them every time you walk into that room for about two weeks. But after a while, they begin to blend in with everything else, and they no longer attract your attention. How to deal with this? Change the color of the sticky note every week or two, or make changes to them when you realize that you are not noticing them as much. Alternatively, change them when you go through a stressful period, when you need them more. Similarly, you may want to change the sound of your auditory cues too. Finally, you may want to switch back and forth from auditory cues to visual cues.

If you have children at home, or you are a teacher, use the sticky notes as reminders to your kids. You might be a little embarrassed that you are putting up these sticky notes all over the house. Certainly children will be asking why you have posted the blue (or whatever color you have chosen) notes all over the place. You can talk to them right after you put them up and tell them that these are reminders to do whatever you want to impress upon them at the time. Then when you change the color, find a new reason. Some examples of reminders it can be for your children: pick up after yourself, be polite, be thankful for what you have, follow the golden rule. The possibilities are endless. I have witnessed situations in which parents are perfectly honest with their children and the children then become more relaxed as a result of looking at the sticky notes and letting go. This can create a positive spiral such that the child is more relaxed. In turn, the parent is less stressed and more pleasant with the child, resulting in the child being better adjusted.

Given the importance of catching stress early, all of the following chapters have a side-bar called "Nip it in the Bud." Each of these side-bars contain a different way in which you can prevent your stress and anxiety from spiraling out of control.

Live It!

1. Catching stress and worry early is the foundation of weakening the old habit of anxiety and worry while strengthening a new habit of being relaxed and in the moment. So do not delay.....

2. Put up sticky notes in places where you will see them most frequently and in places that you associate with stress even if you see them infrequently. Put up no less than ten and as many as thirty. Use them at home, at work, and in your vehicle.

3. When you see the reminders, use relaxation strategies whether you feel like you need to relax or not. It is not necessary to stop what you are doing. In fact, it's usually best if you only stop to relax when you feel you have extra time or when you are particularly stressed.

4. Use mindfulness and other relaxation strategies anytime you become aware that you're stressed or anytime you happen to think about it.

CHAPTER 5

DON'T WORRY, PROBLEM SOLVE

Worrying is using your imagination to create something you don't want.

Before discussing the usefulness of problem solving, I'd like to provide my definition of worrying: Thinking useless thoughts that cause distress (tension, anxiety, fear, irritability, impatience, frustration) without being productive. They are not attempts to problem solve or plan.

An example of a string of three worries is "I'm afraid I'm not going to meet that deadline. This is going to be so stressful. I hope I can get some sleep." There is nothing in those statements that attempts to change things or make things better. These thoughts are useless and they cause distress, so they are worries. In some instances, you may not be aware of actually having specific negative thoughts, but you feel pressure in your chest, knots in your stomach, or some other form of physical stress. It's almost as if your body is worrying without words.

Remember when Bobby McFerrin had the hit single "Don't Worry, Be Happy"? Don't we all wish it were that easy? While it's certainly much more desirable to just "be happy" than to problem solve, it's unrealistic. In this chapter, I explain why people worry, uncover how worrying can actually prevent problem solving, and give you tips on how to problem solve more effectively and thereby reduce worry.

There are at least three reasons why people worry. One is superstition, or a false sense of control. Some examples of this include "I have worried all my life and nothing awful has happened" and "I'm afraid that if I don't worry, something will take me by surprise and go badly." Or it may just be a false sense of control; that is, you feel like worrying somehow gives you more control over your life. The irony is that worrying is more likely to keep you from having control, because worriers tend to be inflexible thinkers. When you are anxious you are less likely to look for solutions to your problems. Worried thoughts are useless thoughts. Only problem solving and planning, not worrying, will give you some control by being prepared.

The second reason people worry is that it is less painful than recounting traumatic memories from their past. It is easier to worry about money, for instance, than to think about how your father beat you, your sister, and your mother.

The third reason, I believe, is the main reason people worry and likely the reason you worry. You are trying to increase the likelihood that good things will happen and decrease the likelihood that bad things will happen. While this is a healthy goal, you often worry instead of trying to solve your problem or maximize your outcomes. You intermittently reinforce your bad habit of worry by occasionally coming up with a helpful idea. In other words, you worry, worry, worry, worry, worry, worry, get a good idea, worry, worry, worry, worry, worry, worry, worry some more, and then you get another good idea, worry, worry, worry, and so on. In the midst of the bad habit of worrying, you intermittently get reinforced with a good idea here and there. Intermittent reinforcement creates the strongest patterns of behavior (including thinking habits) that are most resistant to change. In other words, it's harder to break a habit that is occasionally rewarded than a habit that is always or usually rewarded. It's like amateur golfers who continue to play despite their frustration because they occasionally get reinforced with a great shot. The good news is that you are more likely to come up with a solution if you focus on ways to solve the problem than if you worry and rely on intermittently coming up with good ideas.

Another problem with worriers is that they often try to push the worried thoughts out of their minds because they know that the thoughts are useless. They often spend much of their energy trying to stop thinking about the topic that they are worried about instead of trying to come up with solutions.

A better strategy is to skip the worrying and cut straight to looking for a solution. If you can't find a solution, apply coping strategies such as acceptance that will help the situation to be more comfortable. It's easier to let go of your worries when you know you've done all you can reasonably do to affect the outcome.

At the beginning of this chapter I mentioned worries about a deadline. In this situation an example of problem solving is "I'm going to get it finished, even if it's not great. Then I can go back and perfect it if I have time." Another possible solution is "I can talk to my boss and tell him I know I can improve it if I can have an extra day or two." These are just a couple of possible solutions to the problem.

There are different methods of problem solving. One that combines problem solving with mindfulness is to observe your thoughts. Get a piece of paper and pen or pencil, or sit near a computer. Close your eyes and start to think about the problem at hand. After each thought label it as "productive" or "useless." Make a record of the productive or helpful thoughts. Attempt to solve the problem, but also be accepting and be aware of when you have a worry or a useless thought. You can label these useless thoughts by saying "useless" aloud, writing down the useless thought, or just thinking the label "useless." Your awareness of these thoughts and labeling them as "useless" can automatically cause these thoughts to decrease or even disappear. This leaves more room to allow the problem-solving thoughts to break through. Then you can begin to look for productive thoughts. For more on the mindful observation of thought see Chapter 8: Mindfullness 301 - Acceptance.

Another way to problem solve is to brainstorm all possible solutions without evaluating the utility of these solutions until later. First make a list. For instance, if your landlord won't fix the leaking ceiling despite four or five phone calls over the past couple of months, your list might include:

1. refuse to pay rent until it's fixed
2. write a letter to the landlord
3. write a letter to the Better Business Bureau
4. write a letter to both
5. move out
6. take photos of the leakage
7. document all I am doing
8. call daily until they fix it
9. slap the landlord
10. contact a lawyer
11. have a friend call the landlord and pretend she's a lawyer
12. contact tenant's rights for advice
13. e-mail friends for ideas
14. e-mail friends to see if they have any friends who are landlords and ask them what to do
15. hire someone to fix it and deduct it from the rent
16. fix it myself and deduct it from the rent
17. get an estimate and write the landlord that I am going to have it fixed and deduct it from the rent if it's not fixed by a certain time.

Obviously, some of these ideas are ridiculous and unethical. However, sometimes outrageous ideas trigger thoughts of good ideas. At the least they might help you to laugh. You can also get someone else to brainstorm a list as well, but if you do, have him or her do it separately because research shows that you will actually come up with more ideas if you work independently first. Then you may get ideas based on the ideas of others or combine some of your ideas with theirs. Worriers tend to have myopic thinking - that is, they usually see a limited scope of possibility - therefore this is a good exercise if you are a worrier.

Once your list is made, it may be easy to come to a decision about how to solve the problem. If it isn't, you can use the process of elimination by crossing off the ideas you know aren't good, like slap the landlord. Rate the remaining items on a scale of 1 to 10, with 10 being an excellent idea and 1 being a bad idea. Choose the highest scoring idea, and if you aren't certain consider discussing the feasibility and utility of the ones you like best with someone you respect.

Another way to do problem solving is to actually devote a specific time to problem solve each day so that you are less likely to worry the rest of the day. For example, if you have a long commute to work you might designate one way of your commute to working on problem solving. Then at all other times if you start to get distressed, you (a) remind yourself that you will work on it during your commute, and then (b) use other coping strategies such as focusing on your senses to help you to not worry about it at that time. In some instances, you might devote the travel time both to and from work to problem solving. If you're driving, you might consider using a recording device to provide a record of your ideas, or if you have a lot of stoplights on your drive you can use them as an opportunity to write out your ideas.

If you don't have a long commute to work or you are concerned that you won't do effective problem solving at that time, set aside another time to problem solve. For instance it might be after dinner each night.

Regardless of when and where you do this, make it a specific time or before or after a specific event and stick to it. It will not typically work if you just try to postpone it to an unspecified time. At first you may schedule a session daily, or even twice daily. The goal is to gradually decrease the frequency and length of your problem-solving sessions. For instance, if your worry is centered around work, you may start by worrying on your way to work each day, then go to Monday, Wednesday, Friday, and then Monday and Thursday, and eventually down to zero. Then if a new problem arises that causes more worrying than usual, you can temporarily utilize this strategy again.

One of my favorite coping tools is what I call the two-column technique. I invented this for an individual with severe insomnia who received only mild to moderate improvement in sleep with all of the other tools I provided. This turned out to be the magic key. Within just a few days she was sleeping better than she had in years.

I shared this idea with a colleague who was working with several students at a university. He found a great deal of success utilizing the two-column technique with students who had difficulty concentrating on studying because their worries had interfered. This technique can be used to help you sleep and it can also be used anytime that you think your worries may interfere with concentration, whether it be with studying, working, or being able to enjoy yourself.

The technique is very simple. In the first column, write down what you are likely to worry about when you don't want to be interrupted with worry. For instance, you want to go to sleep, but you are concerned that you will start to worry once you get into bed and turn off the light. Therefore in the first column you will write "What I think I might worry about . . .":

- *before I'm able to fall asleep*
- *while I'm working*
- *while I'm at home with my family after work*
- *while I'm out with my friends*
- *while I'm trying to study*
- *while I'm watching the movie*
- *while I'm reading*
- *OR during any other activity in which you want to be productive, relaxed, or have fun.*

In the second column, write down what you want to do about it before this time period. The second column will have the title "What I'm going to do about it before I . . ."

- *wind down for the evening*
- *start working*
- *leave work*
- *go out with friends*

- study
- watch the movie
- read

There are three possibilities for what you can do about your worry (second column):

1. <u>Do something</u> before you do the thing in which worrying could interfere.

2. <u>Plan to do something</u> sometime after the event in which you're concerned worry might interfere. For the best results, make a record of what you plan to do and when you plan to do it.

3. <u>Do nothing</u>.

The following three charts depict examples of the two-column technique:

What might I worry about after work?	What am I going to do about it before I leave today?
The Stevens Account	Talk to my boss and if she's already gone e-mail her re: my concerns.
	Write a reminder to call Mr. Stevens after the morning meeting.

What might I worry about before bed?	What am I going to do about it before bed?
The rash on Murphy's back.	If it's no better or looks worse tomorrow I'll call the vet.
Money	I won't spend any money tonight.
	Saturday after breakfast, I'll work on a budget and pay bills. (Write it on your calendar.)

What might I worry about while out with friends?	What do I want to do before we go out?
The meeting with my boss tomorrow.	NOTHING!

In the first example the first problem-solving idea was "something" while the second idea was a "plan to do something." The second example with the rash on the dog is a type of planning that is postponing the worry and postponing a decision. It is, nonetheless, a plan to do something: check the dog the next day and call the vet if the rash isn't better.

In the last example, even though the decision was to do nothing, this individual has actually done something. The person considered the options and decided that the best course of action is no action. For example, he may have considered to prepare what he would say to his boss, but decided it wasn't worth the time and energy. He may have considered postponing the meeting, but then realized that it wasn't a good option because it would not please the boss and that it was better to get it out of the way. Just the fact that he has written out the worry and considered options, his choice to do nothing is likely to be helpful in decreasing or eliminating the worry. If you think that you already do this in your head and the benefit is limited, please consider writing it down because we process our thoughts and emotions differently when we write them.

> ### De-Stress, Then Fix the Mess
>
> Michel Dugas and his colleagues found that worriers have no deficit in problem-solving skills. However, anxiety does interfere with the utilization of their skills. This suggests that mindfulness and other forms of relaxation can help to lead you to the answers.

Worriers often try unsuccessfully for hours not to worry. They often find themselves doing a dance, frequently straddling the worry and the moment (i.e., the activity in which they are attempting to engage). Their efforts not to worry, however, prevent problem solving. When this happens, the worry is not resolved and the activity is typically less productive and less enjoyable. Rather than straddling the worry such that you're worrying while trying to be in the present, it is better to give your worry brief and intense consideration to figure out what you can do about it. Once you make a decision to do something, plan something, or not do anything, it will be easier to be in the moment for longer periods of time. In other words, if you feel you are unable to be in the moment because you are worrying or even if you are stressed about something that is in the back of your mind, it may be useful to stop fighting it. It is often helpful to allow it to come to the forefront of your mind and deal with it so that you are able to move on.

Nip It In The Bud

Whether you are a stay-at-home mom or an executive of a major corporation, anytime someone addresses you, whether it is by your first name, "Mom," "Dad," "honey," or "hey you," use it as a reminder to use coping strategies such as mindfulness or problem-solving.

This is particularly useful if you find that you are unable to enjoy yourself in times of leisure or unable to be productive in times that you are working. You may find it useful to stop your activity and problem solve. In other words, be completely in the moment or take the time to give your worry "airtime in your head" where it is the focus of attention. This will actually increase your ability to let go of the stress because you have given the problem due consideration.

If you find that a worry is preventing you from being productive or keeping you from enjoying yourself, give your problem due diligence by trying to solve it. Be willing to go as far as putting your book down, getting out of bed, or excusing yourself and "going to the bathroom" when among friends. Then do the two-column technique in writing or in your head if something to write with is not available. Again, remember that sometimes it is best to write because we process things differently when we write our ideas down instead of just thinking about them. When you are alone, you can try a third way of processing: talking aloud. Finally, if it's appropriate you can process your issue by discussing it with a supportive person. Bottom line, don't worry - problem solve or accept. Anything else is useless and only causes stress and zaps your energy.

Live It!

1. Use the two-column technique if you are concerned that your worries will interfere with sleep or concentration for work or play.

2. Observe your thoughts and label each one as being "productive" or "useless." Make a record of the productive thoughts.

3. If something continues to bother you, brainstorm possible solutions and set up a plan to put those solutions into action or let it go.

Chapter 6

Take a Break

I wish I had a buck for every time I've heard people say that they don't have time to take a break. The fact is that when you feel like you don't have time to take a break, that is probably the time you need it the most. Sometimes, you don't have time to *not* take a break, because efficiency declines with stress and fatigue such that you get further behind than you would have been had you taken a break. Breaks can clear your mind and rejuvenate your soul. Breaks usually lead to such a significant improvement in productivity that you can make up the time you spent on the break in several minutes, thereby accomplishing more in the long run. And the fringe benefit: you get to enjoy the break!

It is a fact that Americans work more hours than in any other country, yet we are the least productive. I believe that Americans are least productive for at least three reasons: (1) we work more hours per week than people in other countries, (2) we get less vacation time, and (3) we have so much more expected of us that we live under the illusion that we have no choice but to keep working despite fatigue. Therefore, we don't have ample opportunities to recharge our batteries such that we become inefficient.

THE PRODUCTIVITY/BREAK CONNECTION

In addition to corporate demands, some people believe that working sixty to ninety hours in a week is some kind of badge of honor. Working that many hours in a week on occasion is usually not very harmful and may be necessary in some graduate programs, internships, and residencies. However, someone who chooses to do it regularly or even frequently is foolish rather than honorable. The problem occurs when people get into the habit of working this hard for years; such a work ethic can have serious effects on physical and emotional health. And what is the point of working so hard if you really aren't able to enjoy life?

There is evidence that we can concentrate for only about fifty minutes at a time. This is part of the reason that the standard therapy hour is forty-five to fifty minutes. This is also why middle school and high school classes are typically about fifty minutes. The ten-minute break tends to rejuvenate and clear the mind, and the student can be refueled for another fifty minutes of study. Furthermore, it is a fact that regardless of what the task is (mental or physical, complex or simple), workers engaged in an eight-hour day actually accomplish significantly less if they work those eight hours without a break than if they work seven hours with one hour of breaks (i.e., eight hours minus four fifteen-minute breaks). How is that possible?

I explain this by using a productivity quotient. The productivity quotient can be defined as a person's average percentage of productivity, with 100 percent being peak performance or the individual's greatest productivity level. If someone works for sixty minutes at 100 percent productivity - his or her peak performance - that person's productivity quotient for the hour is 100 percent. If he or she works half an hour at 100 percent productivity and not at all for half an hour, that person's productivity quotient is 50 percent. If someone works 100 percent for thirty minutes and 50 percent for thirty minutes, his or her productivity quotient is 75 percent.

Now, I'd like for you to think about times that you are working and you are "on." Reflect on those great times when you are on a roll. You are very focused and enjoying peak performance and peak productivity; you are in the moment. Contrast that with memories of being so tired that you aren't thinking quickly or are moving slowly. Also, remember times when you have been so overwhelmed that you aren't able to concentrate or even worse, you freeze and stare into space. Worse still, consider when you are so stressed that you start making mistakes that take more time to undo (this can be defined as a negative productivity level).

At least five behaviors lower productivity. One is being slower: either moving or thinking more slowly. This is probably the least problematic. Another common productivity zapper is a decrease or loss of concentration. Third is doing something that's not really taking a break, but is also not working. One example is surfing the Net for something unimportant just to avoid work, but not enjoying it [see Chapter 12: No Putzing]. Another one is complaining with a colleague. Despite feeling like you were heard, you really don't feel re-energized, because you were talking about work. Finally, the worst hit to productivity is making mistakes that end up costing time and on rare occasions thousands of dollars or more.

Consider the example on the next page in which Worker One takes breaks and Worker Two does not. This is a very likely situation. In fact, I really believe that Worker Two's lack of breaks would affect his productivity even more than I have indicated here.

As you compare the two workers, you might argue that there is not a big difference between 66 percent and 60 percent. Although the workers only differ by 6 percentage points, Worker One was 10 percent more productive. You might still argue that it's insignificant. But think about if you got off of work 10 percent sooner or if you got 10 percent more time to relax, or if you got paid 10 percent more. Now 10 percent seems like a lot more, doesn't it?

In addition to the 10 percent increase in production, consider how much more pleasant Worker One's day was. She enjoyed four breaks in addition to lunch. And she probably felt better while she was working because she felt more productive. Finally, consider the difference in energy levels once the two workers left work. Worker One is likely to feel better about her day, be less stressed at the end of the day, have more energy, and feel greater satisfaction for her accomplishments. Furthermore, Worker One will be able to enjoy her evening more. At the beginning of the next day, Worker

An Example of Productivity With or Without Breaks:

Hour	Worker One *Break-taking Worker*	Worker Two *Worker not taking breaks*
1	90%	90%
2	52.5% (70% for 45 min; 0% for 15 min break)	67.5% (70% for 45 min; 60% for 15 min)
3	75%	50%
4	52.5% (0% for 15 min break; 70% for 45 min)	37.5% (45% for 15 min; 35% for 45 min)
lunch	break	break
5	85%	85%
6	52.5% (70% for 45 min; 0% for 15 min break)	67.5% (70% for 45 min; 60% for 15 min)
7	70%	50%
8	45% (0% for 15 min break; 60% for 45 min)	32.5% (40% for 15 min; 30% for 45 min)
AVG	66%	60%

One is likely to arrive feeling more rested and have a more positive attitude than Worker Two. Therefore, Worker One will probably start the day with a higher productivity level. Consider five days in a row of being Worker One versus being Worker Two. For Worker Two, fatigue and burnout are more likely and by the end of each week the gap between productivity levels is likely to widen.

If you smoke, you probably already take breaks. Although I would never encourage people to smoke, smokers feel entitled to their breaks and are more productive when they return to their desks - and not just because of the nicotine. If you find that you forget to take breaks, you might ask a colleague who smokes to remind you when he or she takes a smoke break. If you happen to be quitting smoking, continue to take breaks. It will probably help you to quit because you won't miss the breaks. However, it's probably best to take a short walk or go into a non-smoking break room, rather than hang out with the smokers where temptation will likely call.

In addition to continuing to use sticky notes to let go of unneeded tension, you can use them to evaluate your productivity level. If your job does not restrict you to take breaks only at specific times, use your productivity level to determine when to take a break. I would recommend that you take a break when your productivity level gets down to between 50 and 70 percent, depending on how productive you consider yourself to be. If you think your average productivity level is high (e.g., 80 to 85 percent), take a break when you get to 65 to 70 percent. If you think your average productivity level is lower than 80 percent, then wait to switch tasks until you get to a level lower than 65 percent.

When taking a break try to avoid talking about work. Also, get away from your desk or the spot from which you are working. Take a mindfulness walk or sit outside and be mindful. Go to the cafeteria if your workplace has one, or go to the break room. You could call or text a friend or check personal e-mail, or read a book or a magazine. Whatever it is you choose to do, see to it that it is relaxing and enjoyable. I do not recommend that you sit at your desk surfing the Net, playing a game, or e-mailing-even if it's your personal e-mail. However, if you have a laptop, Blackberry, iPhone, or other portable device, then it is fine to do these things on your break. The bottom line? Get a change of scenery and do something relaxing, enjoyable, or both.

An alternative to taking breaks is switching tasks. It's best to switch tasks when you are not allowed to take a break in your work or when you really don't want to take a complete break but feel you'd benefit from a diversion. For instance, let's say that you are working on some type of report or a big project at work that takes a long time. You recognize that you are not really tired but that you are losing interest, you are bored, or your brain feels like it has turned to mush. If you don't feel like you really need to take a break, switch tasks. Check your voice mail or your e-mail. Work on a different project. Make some business calls, clean your desk, or do something else productive until you feel you are ready to tackle the first project again.

Vacations and Time for Ourselves

Vacations are another kind of break on a larger scale. I believe it is very important to take vacations because they usually revive you. Typically when you go back to work after a week or more of vacation you feel fresh, relaxed, more willing to work, and seem to enjoy it better while also being more productive.

If at all possible, do not bring any work with you while on vacation - period. This includes e-mail and

Conditioning Your Nose

Recall from Chapter 4 that we can become classically conditioned to smells. If you use a relaxing scent such as lavender only when you are really anxious, you run the risk of causing it to be associated with stress and anxiety, instead of relaxation and peace. You can strengthen the power of the scent if you use it frequently when you are already relaxed.

Try the following three-step strategy:

1.   Choose a scent that you find pleasant. A good deal of science has indicated that lavender, cedarwood, lilac, and jasmine have relaxing properties. Therefore, it's best to choose one of these scents or another one that is considered to be soothing or calming.

2.   When you are meditating, taking a relaxing bath, or otherwise noticing that you are relaxed, make an effort to smell this scent. If you are stressed before you start engaging in a relaxing activity, wait until you have already begun to feel relaxed to smell the scent. Do this at least five times before going onto step 3..

3.   Carry the scent with you and when you begin to feel stressed, sniff it. Be sure to continue to pair this pleasant scent with relaxation to keep the positive calming association strong.

phones that are tied to work. A compromise is to take work to do only on the plane or perhaps deal with e-mails and phone calls the last day of the trip or on only one day in the middle of the trip. It's not truly a vacation if you work most of the days, even if it's only for a short period of time. It's best to get 100 percent away from work.

If you have difficulty with the re-entry and don't feel revived after a vacation, it may mean that you could benefit from some major life changes. It might be that it's not a week or two weeks of vacation that you needed, but a permanent vacation from your job or your lifestyle. This may be particularly true if you do not like the people you work for and with, if the demands on time and productivity are very unreasonable, or if you are a stay-at-home mom (especially with preschoolers) or a full-time caretaker for a live-in relative. In the latter situations you may need to hire someone to give you breaks or arrange quiet times if your children don't take naps.

If, on the other hand, you know that you like your job and you want to continue what you're doing, I would recommend that you take some time when you return from your vacation to settle into home before rushing off to work the next day. I follow this general rule: for each week that you are away spend one day at home before going back to work. For example, if you are gone for a four-day weekend, I'd recommend that you come home by 2:00 or 3:00 in the afternoon the day before you go back to work. If you are gone for a week, come home two nights before you have to go back to work (i.e., if you are returning to work on a Monday, get home Saturday night, even if it's late).

Some people argue that they want to get every minute they can out of their vacation, so they plan to come home late Sunday night after being gone for a week or two. They return to eight messages on their home machine, stacks of mail, piles of laundry, and other unpacking to be done. Then they may have pictures they want to process, edit, and sort. Although they get that extra day on vacation, they pay for it by coming home immediately behind and stressed out by these responsibilities.

If you find you feel like you aren't revived from your vacations and typically return from your vacation the night before you go back to work, imagine what it would be like if you sacrificed that one day per week of vacation and cut your vacation short. Come home from a one-week vacation and sleep in your own bed on, say, Saturday night. The next morning you can throw in some laundry, have a leisurely breakfast, sort through the mail, decide which phone calls you want to make today and which you may want to put off. You can go through the pictures you took and enjoy working with them and easily make them a "want to" rather than a task that you feel obliged to do. If you'd like you could even find some time to go grocery shopping. By late afternoon or early evening you can be finished with unpacking, mail, laundry, and most of your other tasks, and then do something fun or relaxing. Let your vacation continue that evening by going out to dinner, seeing a movie, or getting together with some friends for a drink and show them your photos.

Another issue that some people have is not taking enough time to be alone and have quiet time. Similarly, couples often don't take enough time together without family and friends. On Monday, for example, you may work and then run errands, Tuesday you work and go out with friends, Wednesday you work and do chores around the house, and on Thursday you go to work and hang out with family, and then the weekend comes and you do laundry and tend to the lawn and hang out with friends.

> **Nip It in the Bud**
>
> Do you have pets? If so, use them as reminders. This is a great one because people love their pets. Fido and Fluffy are more likely to be stress relievers than stress inducers. Anytime they "ask" for your attention, use it as a reminder to let go of unneeded tension or to ask yourself if you could use a break. In addition, pet your animals or watch them as a mindfulness activity. For instance, watching fish is a wonderful mindfulness activity.

Sometimes it's best to just lie on the couch and watch a movie, read a book, or spend time with a hobby such as painting or playing music. The biggest mistake we make here is by always making work a priority. The second most likely mistake is that someone asks us if we are free on a certain date and we make a commitment even when we'd rather have downtime.

Whether your life is out of balance because you are always making work a priority or you accept nearly every social engagement unless you're booked, scheduling time for yourself or a date night with your spouse will allow you to make it as important of a priority as work or plans with others. If someone inquires about getting together at that time you say, "I'm sorry, I'm busy that night." The individual doesn't need to know that you're busy watching a movie at home by yourself or have a date with your spouse or partner. Alternatively, if it is something you (or you and your date) really want to do, accept the invitation and make it a point to reschedule the "alone date" just before or just after that. Scheduling alone time with or without a companion is an important component to leading a more balanced life.

Live It!

1. **Experiment with breaks.** Live your life the way that you have been living it every other day and take breaks on alternate days. On "break days" when you feel that your productivity level is waning, get away from your desk or other place of work; consider leaving the building. Take at least ten minutes, preferably fifteen to twenty minutes, to do something you enjoy. Do this three to eight times in an eight-hour day.

2. At the end of each day rate your level of productivity and think about how much you have accomplished. Also rate how enjoyable your day was, as well as how you feel about starting your next day of work.

3. **Experiment with fewer yet longer breaks** (e.g., three or four twenty-minute breaks) versus many short breaks (e.g., six or eight ten-minute breaks).

Chapter 7

Be Focused

Sometimes people have the opposite problem of spending too much time on one project without taking a break. Instead, they are easily distracted and jump around from task to task. They work on a project for only a few minutes, or sometimes only seconds, before being distracted by checking e-mail, answering the phone, or acting on an impulse to catch up on gossip with a colleague. They may start several things before one task is finished.

Some people have both problems. That is, sometimes they may not take a break when they need it and other times they switch tasks frequently, jumping around from task to task for hours. They may get frustrated because they accomplish very little despite being very busy and stressed.

When you jump from task to task your ability to focus is limited. Moreover, you will often lose your momentum and lose your place. This wastes valuable time that is taken to reorient to each task that had temporarily been abandoned. Unless your job is to take phone calls and respond immediately to e-mails, it will behoove you to set some boundaries with interruptions - both interruptions that are self-imposed and those that are a result of other people interrupting you.

Consider the following scenario:

Bill arrives at work at 9:00 a.m. and starts to write a letter. The phone rings and he answers it. While talking to the caller he tells her that he will write an e-mail to someone about scheduling a meeting. He goes into e-mail to write the note and sees that there are a couple of other e-mails in his in-box from early this morning. He answers those before he writes the e-mail he set out to write. At 9:25 he goes back to the letter he started at 9:00 a.m. and has to reread what he started writing twenty-five minutes ago. Just as he starts to write he hears he has a new e-mail. This makes him realize that he forgot to write the e-mail he had agreed to write a few minutes ago when he got sidetracked by the two new e-mails. He starts to write it and someone comes by his desk and asks him a question. He talks to that person for a few minutes, then has to reorient to the e-mail, having to reread what he wrote, and just before he finishes it, the phone rings, he answers it, and has to go into another file to answer the question. But before he does that, he goes to get a cup of coffee. When he comes back he sees that he has a phone message, so he listens to the message and returns the call. Then he goes back to the file where he is to write the letter-once again reorienting to what he wrote. Before he finishes the letter he has to use the restroom. 10:30: He comes back from the restroom and again reorients to what he's writing; he gets another e-mail and opens it before finishing the letter. Then he sees that he didn't finish that e-mail he had agreed to send before the phone rang about an hour ago. After rereading what he had already written, he finishes the e-mail and sends it. He once again reorients to the letter he started at 9:00 a.m., but before he finishes, someone comes by his desk and interrupts with a question. He interrupts the conversation because he sees that his boss is on the line . . . wondering where the letter is. He can't believe that he started working on this first thing in the morning and it's now after 11:00 a.m. and the letter still isn't finished. He feels overwhelmed and frustrated.

Now consider the following revision to how Bill could work more efficiently if he set boundaries on how he deals with the phone, e-mail, and other interruptions. He puts a headset on now to limit who will interrupt him. He could even put a note on the back of his chair that says: Do Not Disturb.

Bill arrives at work at 9:00 a.m. and starts to write a letter. The phone rings and he allows it to go into voice mail. He has the e-mail alert on his computer turned off so that he's not even aware that he got an e-mail. Someone comes by his desk and sees that he is working and has headphones on and, instead of interrupting him, phones him. Bill allows the call to go to voice mail. At 9:40 he finishes the letter. He enjoys a sense of accomplishment. He rewards himself and goes to get a cup of coffee. He checks his voice mail and takes notes on his messages. He responds to the first one by writing an e-mail to the desired fellow and rather than calling this caller back, he copies her on the e-mail she had requested. He saw that there were two other e-mails in his box from this morning, but he resists the urge to read them until he addresses the concerns of the woman who came by his desk earlier. He realizes it will likely be quicker to send her an e-mail than to call her or go by her desk. 10:00 a.m.: He begins to answer the first of the two e-mails. A few minutes later the phone rings, so he quickly finishes the e-mail before picking up and does so on the third ring; he gets the requested info and gives it to the person. He opens the second e-mail from earlier that morning. As he is responding he sees another message come in and temporarily ignores it. 10:30: He finishes the e-mail and goes to the restroom. He answers the last e-mail when he returns. He has not wasted time reorienting and switching tasks and is caught up by 10:45. And he never has to field that call from his boss because the letter was finished in a timely manner.

It's easy to see how jumping around from task to task and allowing all possible interruptions results in wasted time from having to refocus time after time. You probably noticed too that the second scenario felt more relaxed. Not only does Bill finish at 10:45 instead of finding himself with more work to do after 11:00, but he's also going to feel better and have more energy to be productive through his day. Furthermore, his boss received the letter at least ninety minutes earlier and without having to ask for it.

There are several distractions that can keep you from really focusing on your work. Many are external, that is, from other people via the phone, e-mail, or in person. Some of these distractions are mandatory, like meetings and conference calls. However, depending on the nature of your job, some distractions are very much under your control. For instance, rather than letting the phone interrupt you and throw you off track, you have the option of putting the phone directly into voice mail. You can also set your e-mail so that you are not alerted to new messages and turn off instant messenger. You can put a "Do Not Disturb" sign on the back of your chair if you work in a cubicle or on your door if you are fortunate enough to have one.

You might have a profession or job in which you feel a need to be available immediately when possible. If you are an administrative assistant, for instance, you may have no choice but to answer the phone right away. Similarly, I know stockbrokers, real-estate agents, real-estate appraisers, and many self-employed people in various businesses feel it is important to be readily available. There is a difference if your job description requires you to answer the phone and e-mail immediately, but you can still control your interruptions.

If you are a secretary or in customer service, for instance, you may be required or strongly urged to pick up the phone as soon as possible. However, you might be able to let e-mails stack up for an hour or more. Furthermore, you might be able to set your e-mail so that you are only alerted that you have mail when it's from specific people to whom you may want or need to respond rapidly. Alternatively, you could send out a memo, or discuss in a meeting, telling people to phone you if they have an issue that's urgent and to e-mail you for everything routine.

If necessary, discuss some of this with your manager or supervisor. If you present it in the right way, any reasonable supervisor should be grateful that you are trying to be more productive. Here's an example of what you might say: "Dr. Mallory, I've been reading a book on how to be more productive and it suggests that people lose productivity because they keep switching tasks and spend too much time between tasks and reorienting. I was thinking that when I'm writing a letter for you, it would be most efficient for me to allow calls to go into my voice mail and then return the calls as soon as I'm finished with the letter." If your boss refuses, at least you know you tried! And feel better by thinking something like, "My boss does my evaluations and partially determines my raises. Apparently, he values my immediate response to the phone and e-mail more than being efficient."

If you have a profession in which people expect you to be available and your success depends on it, you might feel that these suggestions do not apply to you. In such a case, you can certainly decide that your well-being might be worth it to make some compromises. What I suggest in this case is to be available most of the time, but allow yourself to have some instances in which you are not available. I recommend two general ways to do this: (1) take a break the same time each day and let it be known to your clients or customers, and (2) be mindful of when you really need that break emotionally or want to focus on accomplishing an important task and be willing to take a few minutes away from the phone.

It can be very helpful to have a time period or two during the day that you are not available. You can let people know when you will be doing this on your voice mail. You're unlikely to lose business if people know they only have to wait about an hour or so for a return call. Consider taking this time when you are least likely to get calls. Or in the spirit of the last chapter, take breaks at a time of day that you feel you are least productive and/or when you are most likely to really want a break. For instance, you may want to take an hour for lunch and not be bothered by calls. If you receive many calls during the lunch hour, opt for a late or early lunch. Your voice mail might say something like "I will be unavailable for calls between 1 and 2 each day. I will check my messages at 2 p.m. and return all calls accordingly."

When you feel that you could really benefit from taking a break for yourself or that you'd really like to put some concentrated time in on a project be willing to not answer the phone. In such case, if you are worried about losing business or disgruntling clients you could leave a message something like this "I'm sorry I'm not available to take your call. I do check my messages frequently and usually return calls within an hour or two, but typically sooner."

In addition to the external distractions that we contend with in phone calls, e-mails, and so forth, there are many self-distractions. Some are biological, some are social, some may be personal business, and some are emotional. These distractions include using the restroom, eating, getting coffee or another beverage, making phone calls, writing e-mails, and choosing to talk to colleagues in person. The key is to shelter yourself from these distractions and then use them as a break or as a diversion. For instance, you might be

> **Nip It in the Bud**
>
> Anytime you do switch tasks, use it as a reminder to loosen your body, breathe, or change your perspective. When you switch rooms, leave a building, enter a building, or get in or out of your car, nip your stress in the bud.

Teams

If you are one of the many people who work on a team, either where everyone does the same thing or where you are each from a different department working on the same project, you may have more solutions to your productivity problem. Be creative about how you can be more productive as a team. Try taking turns being in the "hot seat" for taking calls, handling e-mails, or other interruptions inherent in your job. This will allow one or more people to enjoy the "cold seat" where they are last in line for interruptions and have more opportunity to finish projects without interruptions. This can also help to break up the monotony of the day if you divide it into half days or two-hour segments, for example. You may even divide the types of interruptions according to strengths, the specific demands of the day, or even according to individual preferences of tasks. This will almost certainly increase productivity as well as satisfaction.

One work team I know about actually uses small items that are placed on top of their cubes to indicate their status. They creatively came up with "Ghost" as the person who gets to be free of interruptions for that period to catch up on work projects. They assigned the name "It" to the person on the front line to be responsible for all calls unless already on another call and for all the other small spur-of-the-moment tasks required of the team. The "Ghost" only picks up calls if the others are all already on the phone. Others on the team would take over the tasks only if "It" is on the phone. To do this for your group, find a toy ghost (always available around Halloween) and put that on the cube of the person who is to be treated as if he or she is not there unless absolutely necessary. If you can't find a ghost, a small white stuffed animal will work just as well. Then place a bright colored stuffed animal on the cube of each person who is "It." They are on the front line and are the first to get calls or other work that requires interruptions. Alternatively, you could simply put up signs or anything red to indicate the "hot seat" and anything blue to indicate the "cold seat."

working on a letter and know you only have a few more minutes to complete it, but you feel an urge to use the restroom. Finish the letter and then go. Another example is that you're working on a report and for some reason you remember to make an appointment for an oil change. If you're afraid you will forget, rather than stopping your flow to call for the appointment, jot it on a note so that you won't forget and won't interrupt your flow. Get in the habit of writing these notes in the same place whether it's on a sticky note that sits next to your computer keyboard, a place on your computer, or in a sticky note list [see Chapter 15].

I also believe that with technology, we are often too connected and could use more time away from it. You may not even be aware of how much time you spend texting, talking on the phone, and answering e-mails. It's not healthy to be too connected. Periodically do things without taking your phone with you, or if you feel a need to have it for safety reasons, turn it off occasionally. I hear people say they need to have it on in case their kids need them. Our kids will survive if they can't reach us for a couple of hours. After all, people survived before the advent of cell phones.

Part of the wonderful thing about a real vacation is that, if you choose to, you can be away from the phone and e-mail. Experiment with taking one day per week, or even a half day per week, free of them. See if it doesn't bring some peace. Also, if it makes you very anxious to do this, you might have an unhealthy addiction to technology. If so, taking some time away from it periodically would be a very good idea. Even though it may make you feel uncomfortable now, you might learn to enjoy the peace of being away.

Live It!

Stay on task. If you are afraid that you will forget to do certain things, keep sticky notes or a notepad nearby or on your computer. If your job allows, close your e-mail so that you do not hear e-mails coming in, and allow your phone to go straight to voice mail at times that you feel it's beneficial to keep your focus on a task.

Chapter 8

Mindfulness 301 - Acceptance

Awareness cures; trying fails.

- Eloise Ristad

About ten years ago a friend of mine told me about a book called *Going to Pieces Without Falling Apart: A Buddhist Perspective on Wholeness; Lessons from Meditation and Psychotherapy,* by David Epstein, a Jewish psychiatrist who practices Buddhism. This is a great book, particularly if you like philosophy, but it's not an easy read. While I was in the process of reading this book I was seeing a client whom I will call "Jane." One particular session with Jane completely transformed how I do therapy and aroused a new level of excitement about treating people who suffer from excessive anxiety. I had been practicing mindfulness for about a decade, but this experience took my mindfulness teachings and practice to a completely new level.

Jane suffered from severe panic attacks several times per week. Her anxiety was so excessive that she had difficulty making it to her therapy sessions. She frequently canceled or arrived very late. Fortunately, in the prior session I had gently confronted her, expressing my concern that she was not going to improve if she could not be more consistent about her appointments. Had I not done so, she likely would have canceled this day that transformed her life and thereby the way that I do therapy.

That afternoon she arrived to her session late and was in the midst of a full-blown panic attack. She sat on the edge of my couch, hyperventilating, crying, and barely able to speak. It took her a couple of minutes just to tell me that she almost didn't come because she was so upset. She also informed me that she was too upset to talk.

My response was that it was okay and I gave her permission not to talk. I suggested that we engage in relaxation. She refused, saying that there was no way she could possibly relax. I agreed that she was probably way too anxious to be able to benefit from relaxation. Nonetheless, I was momentarily befuddled. I had this woman in my office crying, hyperventilating, and hysterical. She had refused my suggestion to engage in relaxation and said she was too upset to talk. I thought, "What am I going to do? Sit here and watch her panic?"

Fortunately, I quickly returned to the peak zone [see Chapter 2]. It was also fortunate that Dr. Epstein's book was fresh in my mind. What I did is not borrowed from David Epstein; rather I was inspired by his Buddhist-influenced work. I developed what I learned from Dr.

Epstein into a technique for reducing anxiety and frustration. Since then I have learned that many other therapists use similar forms of mindful acceptance in their practice.

Sitting there with Jane, I transformed the concepts I had learned from Dr. Epstein into a therapeutic technique of sorts. I said something like, "Okay, I'm not going to try to engage you in relaxation, but would you be willing to close your eyes?" And with that she did. The essence of what I said went something like this: "Observing where you feel the discomfort in your body. Observing it almost as if you're an outsider looking in on the discomfort. Noticing where the discomfort is located. Feeling how much space it takes up in your body. Don't try to change it, but if it changes, allowing it to change. If it increases, let it increase, and if it decreases, let it decrease. Just continuing observing it and noticing how it feels. Letting go of the struggle. Letting go of any judgments about how you feel. Just observing how you feel and accepting it, even though it's uncomfortable." Her response was amazing!

Within two minutes Jane was grinning from ear to ear. She went from tears and hyperventilation to a big smile and then excitement about this rapid transformation from terror to feeling fine, even happy. To my knowledge she never had an unexpected panic attack again and had very infrequent situational panic attacks. When she did have them they were significantly less severe and much shorter than she had suffered prior to this amazing session. Jane was accepting of these panic attacks because they were always in very stressful situations and still much more mild and shorter than they had been in the past. Most of this success was due to less than two minutes of acceptance therapy.

You may have noticed that Jane's spiral was very much advanced and that her SUDS rating was clearly a 10. Jane's story might appear to completely contradict Chapter 4 about early cue detection. Actually, I still contend that coping strategies work best at the earliest events in the spiral - even acceptance. Moreover, while most strategies are no match to high levels of stress and are useless, acceptance is an exception. In fact, it might be the only exception other than drugs. Acceptance can work even when your stress spiral has a great deal of momentum, and it can work faster than medication without side effects.

Since the early 1990s, long before I read Dr. Epstein's book, I had been studying mindfulness as a relaxation tool. Interestingly, I had read a book back in the 1980s when I was in music school called *A Soprano on Her Head*. This book by Eloise Ristad provides tools and insights helpful for musicians who have performance anxiety or are looking to improve their musical skills in a unique way. The opening quote in this chapter, "*Awareness cures, trying fails,*" was found in this book.

I will never forget applying Ristad's advice while I practiced piano. I was working on a very difficult phrase with which I repeatedly made mistakes and often had to stop because I blew it so badly. Her advice in dealing with a frustrating phrase was to play the difficult phrase and simply watch the mistakes. The first time I tried this, I played the phrase beautifully with no mistakes. I thought it was magic. Looking back, her suggestion accomplished two things: (1) it gave me the permission to fail, thereby taking the pressure off, and (2) it put me in the present because I was watching and listening to what I was doing rather than looking to my future fear of making mistakes. In short, I accepted my difficulties with that phrase rather than trying desperately to play it right.

Despite my positive experiences with acceptance in the early '80s, I only began to understand the full utility of the concept when I read Epstein's book near the beginning of the twenty-first century and found the stunning effect it had on Jane.

Doubtless you had heard about the concept of mindfulness before opening this book. Since I read *Going to Pieces Without Falling Apart*, the Buddhist idea of acceptance has become much more mainstream, so it's likely you've heard about the concept of acceptance as well. If nothing else you've probably heard it in the serenity prayer that we often think of as a Christian contribution. Therefore, if you are Christian you

Nip It in the Bud

Use any bodily drive as a reminder to use relaxation. Rather than using all of them, perhaps choose ones that occur most frequently. These drives include, but are not limited to, craving a cigarette, thirst, hunger, needing to use the restroom, and feeling sleepy.

If you drink a lot of fluid, put a colorful rubber band or sweatband around your cup or water bottle to help remind you to be in the moment each time you take a sip. If you are a smoker, simply put a sticky note in each cigarette pack, or put a rubber band around your lighter. Or you can just try to remember that each time you are hungry or crave something to eat to use acceptance or another strategy.

may be more comfortable with the serenity prayer than with acceptance as a Buddhist principle. However, you certainly do not need to be Christian to find benefit from and live the serenity prayer:

*God, grant me the serenity to accept
the things I cannot change,
The strength to change the things I can,
and the wisdom to know the difference.*

Similarly, a lot of people of faith rely on being able to "give it over to God." This is another way of relinquishing emotional strife and stress; put it in God's hands. Even if you believe in the power of prayer, emotionally giving it over to God is a form of acceptance that can immediately reduce your distress.

You may have tried to be accepting without any luck. Many people have difficulty with acceptance because they misunderstand the concept of it. They might think or say, "I don't want to accept it; I want to change it or get rid of it." Be very clear about this: Acceptance does not mean that you are not going to try to change the situation. But when you are looking for solutions you will have more focus, patience, and creativity if you also accept uncomfortable feelings and situations. In fact, Carl Rogers, a famous psychologist, once said, "The curious paradox is that when I accept myself just as I am, then I can change." With combining change and acceptance, I have made an addition to the serenity prayer:

God, grant me the serenity to accept
the things I cannot change,
The strength to change the things I can,
the wisdom to know the difference, and ...
The serenity to accept the things I'm in
the process of changing or
am not yet ready to change.

Acceptance doesn't mean that you need to think positively. Actually, acceptance does not require words at all. However, negative thoughts will certainly prevent you from accepting things. Therefore, in some instances, particularly if you are having difficulty with acceptance, changing your thinking can help to open the door to making acceptance possible.

For example, after having something frustrating happen to you, thinking "This is unfortunate, but it isn't going to do me any good to get upset about it" or "In this type of stressful situation, it's not unusual to be stressed out," may help you to accept your misfortune or at least your reactions to your misfortune. Negative thoughts can make it impossible to accept. Think of the negative alternative: "I can't believe this is happening to me. This is awful! Geez, this is so stressful and I'm not dealing with it well. Oh, I hate the way this feels. I need to try to relax." Thoughts such as these will only cause you more stress and interfere with attempts to be accepting.

Not only do negative thoughts make it more difficult to be accepting, but learning to be more accepting is likely to improve the nature of your thoughts.

For instance, when Jane experienced relief, she smiled and then said what she was thinking. It was something like, "I felt the permission to feel what I was feeling and so I stopped beating myself up. Now I know that it is okay to have some feelings of distress and it doesn't need to be awful."

Probably the single best way to describe acceptance of emotion and physical sensations of anxiety is to simply have you focus on how your stress feels in your body. If you can observe that heavy feeling in your chest or that knot in your stomach (or whatever it is for you) and refrain from reacting to it in a negative way, then you have accepted it.

TO ILLUSTRATE HOW THIS WORKS, THE NEXT TIME YOU ARE FEELING STRESSED, LISTEN TO TRACK 4. OR IF YOU HAVE CHOSEN NOT TO PURCHASE THE RECORDING, READ AND RESPOND TO THE FOLLOWING TEXT OR RECORD IT YOURSELF AND LISTEN:

Observing where you feel discomfort. Noticing how it feels. Observing how much space it takes up. Letting go of any judgments about how it feels. Noticing where it is located. Noticing the texture of how it feels. Letting go of any efforts to try to change it, but if it changes allow it to change. If it increases, allow it to increase, and if it decreases allow it to decrease. If you could see it, what would it look like? Doing the opposite of trying to change it. Don't try to push it away and don't try to make it stay. Giving up any struggle. Just observing it as if you're an outsider looking in.

There are two general things to learn to accept. First is the situation itself. Second is your reaction to it. For instance, you spill coffee on your new pants. You can curse, blame yourself for being clumsy, get frustrated, and be really ticked off that your pants are stained. Or you can accept that there is nothing you can do to change the fact that you spilled the coffee. In this situation, I like to ask, "What would you prefer? Would you rather spill coffee on your pants or spill coffee on your pants, be really upset by it, and let it ruin your morning or even your day?" In this particular example it is really best to accept the situation. In addition, acceptance doesn't mean that you just leave the coffee on your pants. To the contrary, if you are accepting that this accident happened, it is likely you will be quicker with problem-solving strategies (again, the peak zone) and take action that might save your new pants. You will also save a lot of energy you'd waste by getting upset over something that you cannot change and that in the grand scheme of things is not all that important.

However, it's certainly natural that you would feel annoyed by having spilled the coffee. If you are unable to accept the situation and you find that you are upset and you feel powerless to control your frustration, my next question is, "Would you rather be frustrated or would you rather be frustrated and frustrated that you're frustrated?" Therefore, if you can't accept the situation and feel frustrated as a result, accept the frustration rather than getting more frustrated and possibly adding layers of additional emotions onto that. For example, you might start to get anxious that you're frustrated and depressed that you're anxious and frustrated. So find some level of emotion that you are able to accept to prevent the additional layers of reactions.

Acceptance is helpful with many emotions. I work primarily with people who are suffering from anxiety disorders, which is why I first found amazing success with this technique for someone having a panic attack. But acceptance can work just as well with frustration, job tension, family stress, sadness, and many other problems. Not only is it unnecessary to experience the level of distress that Jane did for this technique to be effective, but also it will be more likely to work if your emotions are mild to moderate.

Earlier in this chapter you observed your feelings as a form of acceptance. In Chapter 5 you learned how to observe and label your thoughts as part of a technique to problem solve. However, some people find that by just observing their thoughts, almost as if they are an outsider "witnessing" the thoughts, their minds clear of their own accord. Others find that doing this is useless and may even increase the thoughts, but many find that adding objective labels to their thoughts automatically frees the mind.

WHEN YOU ARE WORRIED, HAVING NO EXPECTATIONS AT ALL, LISTEN TO TRACKS 5 AND 6. ALTERNATIVELY, RECORD OR READ THE FOLLOWING SCRIPTS:

Track 5: *Purposefully begin to think about something that you have been worried about that you have wanted to stop thinking about. (pause) Observing the thoughts that are going on in your mind. (pause) From here on out don't try to think and don't try to not think. Instead, being a passive* *observer by just noticing the thoughts that are going on in your mind without judgment. You may be inclined to try to think or you may be inclined to try to put the thoughts out of your mind. Do neither. Letting go of all effort except to just observe and accept any thoughts that go through your mind. Observing these thoughts almost as if you're an outsider looking in, almost as if you're watching cars drive down the street or birds flying by. (Do this for a minute or two.)*

Track 6: *Observing the thoughts that are going on in your mind. Soon I'm going to ask you to label each thought that you have as being either "new" or "repeat": "repeat" if you've had the thought before, "new" if it's a new or unique thought. If you're not certain, don't get stuck on deciding; rather label it "new" or "pass." If you're alone, label aloud. Do this for a few minutes or until your mind feels settled.*

Often after labeling a thought as "repeat" several times, worriers begin to experience their thoughts in a new way. One in which they not only know in their mind that repetitive worries are useless, but they finally feel the futility of their worry like they've never felt before. The result is often that the worries leave involuntarily and the mind goes blank, moves toward pleasant images, or moves toward the senses. You can use other labels besides "new" and "repeat." You can use "wanted" and "unwanted," "pleasant" and "unpleasant," "worry" and "other," or "useful," "useless," and "neutral." There are numerous other possibilities. Use what feels right to you.

This concept of mindful acceptance is one that I have found can come very easily, but often requires significant effort. Some people are not able to benefit from it. I think there are two reasons why acceptance is challenging. The first is that those who are unable to benefit are still trying to make the discomfort go away and unable to relinquish that struggle. It's the struggle that will often fuel the discomfort. Although they are trying to accept it, they are more focused on making it go away. It won't work if you try to make it go away or get frustrated that it's not going away. If you are doing this, you are not accepting it. In fact, you're doing the opposite of accepting it.

Another reason people have a difficult time grasping this experience of acceptance is that the process is wordless and it is not visual; it's more kinesthetic and emotional. Someone can show you and tell you how to drive a car. I can show you and tell you how to breathe in a relaxing way, but acceptance is different. Words, pictures, and diagrams are sometimes inadequate to explain the experience of acceptance. The other concepts in this book are much more easily conveyed because I am able to specifically explain the approach in a concrete and clear manner with words. In a way teaching acceptance is like trying to explain color to someone who can only see black and white.

METAPHORS AND EXAMPLES

You will probably need to come across a trying situation before you know whether or not you are able to benefit from acceptance. Once you have had a chance to experiment you should know rather quickly whether you are able to accept your emotions or not. For those who struggle with this concept and eventually gain an ability to accept, I have found that different examples and metaphors are often the key to grasping the process. If you have found that acceptance works for you, then it is okay to skip to the next chapter. However, if you feel you are having difficulty being able to accept your emotions, the following examples, photos, and metaphors may help you to internalize the concept of acceptance and use it effectively.

Metaphor One: The Chinese Finger Trap

My mentor on my postdoctoral fellowship at *Penn State*, Tom (T. D. Borkovec), used two examples to explain acceptance and illustrate the utility of it. One example is the Chinese finger trap. Below is a photo of the Chinese finger trap. You can see the tightness of the struggle. The harder one tries to pull his or her fingers apart the more stuck one becomes. Relief is experienced only from giving up the struggle; relief is realized from surrendering. Many of us feel that surrendering is quitting or leaving us vulnerable.

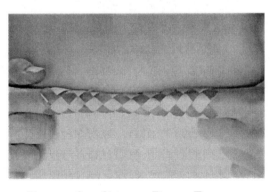

Photo of a Chinese Finger Trap

Not only is this untrue, but often the alternative is to continue a useless struggle that only makes matters worse. Furthermore, with anxiety and with the Chinese finger trap, once we accept it we are more relaxed and thereby in a better position to be able to let go (escape the finger trap) or deal with the situation. Acceptance will help to bring you out of the red zone and into the peak zone.

METAPHOR TWO: BEES

The second metaphor Tom used was of bees. Say you are sitting outdoors and five or six bees are swarming around you. Depending on your experiences in the past you are likely to have at least a small degree of discomfort about the bees. If you surrender, the bees will not likely sting you and they might even settle down a bit if you settle down first. If you start to swat at the bees or try to kill them, you are much more likely to aggravate them. They will fly faster and buzz louder. Not only will this exacerbate your distress, but also you certainly will increase the risk that they will ultimately sting you.

METAPHOR THREE: THE DEVIL'S SNARE

Given that acceptance is a difficult concept to learn, I'd like to give you a fantastic example from a film. In the first Harry Potter film, *Harry Potter and the Sorcerer's Stone*, Harry, Hermione, and Ron find themselves in a position where they need to make a steep jump to safety and find themselves trapped in the roots of a tree. Shortly after the struggle, Hermione is released beneath the roots rather quickly while the other two continue to struggle. Here is the transcript of what happens next:

Hermione: *Stop moving, both of you! This is Devil's Snare. You have to relax! If you don't it'll only kill you faster!*

Ron: *Kill us faster? Oh, now I can relax! (Ron struggles harder, causing him to be grasped more tightly)*

Ron and Harry: *Hermione!*

Ron: *Oh, now what are we going to do?*

Hermione: *Just relax!*

Harry: *Hermione, where are you?*

Hermione: *Do what I say! Trust me!*

(Harry is able to relax and falls free from the roots)

Ron: *Ah! Harry! Harry! (Ron continues to struggle)*

Hermione: *Are you okay?*

Harry: *Yeah, yeah, I'm fine.*

Hermione: *He's not relaxing, is he?*

Ron: *(still struggling) Help!*

Harry: *Apparently not.*

Ron continued to struggle until Hermione remembered that the Devil's Snare weakens with bright light and they are able to free him. Stress and anxiety are often similar to the Devil's Snare such that the more one struggles to escape, the more the person is bound by it. Some people are able to accept and relax despite intense circumstances, much like Hermione and Harry; others, unfortunately, are more like Ron, fighting it only to feel worse.

METAPHOR FOUR:
MY FIRST CHARLEY HORSE

Most people have experienced a charley horse (a painful cramp in the calf). I can remember the first time I got one. I was a little girl, probably about six or seven years old. I was playing on the sidewalk about five feet from our back door. Suddenly I felt this gripping, intense pain in my calf. I was terrified! I screamed. I cried. I was afraid that there was something horribly wrong with my leg. My mom came running out to see what was wrong and when I told her she said something like, "Oh, Jennifer, that's just a charley horse. It's normal. Sometimes people will get a cramp in their leg that hurts really bad, but it's nothing to be worried about." From then on, I accepted calf cramps. They hurt every bit as bad, but they never again scared me and I have never cried or screamed about them since that day. Once you have accepted the pain it's easier to make the cramps go away by stretching those muscles by pointing your toes toward your head.

If you have experienced these cramps you know how painful they can be, but I doubt that they cause you much stress despite how uncomfortable they are. They are more physically painful than any anxiety or frustration symptom you could have. Therefore, when you have those uncomfortable physical sensations of stress in your body, accept them the way you would accept a charley horse and they are very likely to decrease or even go away. It is this response of observing the discomfort and accepting it that can help to decrease the intensity of our stress. However, like the serenity prayer, there are some things we may want to change. And as I have mentioned before, getting out of the red zone and into the peak zone will lead to better problem solving. That is, acceptance will actually help you to change it because you will be more relaxed and more open to ideas and problem solving.

This is the same with other stressors, whether you are stuck in traffic, dealing with an ethical dilemma, or having difficulties with a supervisor or a friend. If you accept the situation and accept the emotions that this causes you to have, you will be less likely to get really stressed. But if you focus on the situation, continue to think negatively, and try to fight healthy emotions, you will end up focusing on both the situation and your feelings about the situation in a negative way. Rather than accepting your healthy emotions and accepting what you can't change, you make an unfortunate situation worse. You waste useful energy and get stressed about being stressed.

Residual Chronic Tension

One thing that might not go away as a result of acceptance is tension in your muscles, because sometimes people have so much built-up tension in their shoulders (or other muscle groups) that they will still ache even after accepting the tension 100 percent. In this case, acceptance should still alleviate some of the stress and help to prevent it from getting worse. If you suffer from chronic muscle tension consider learning progressive relaxation, getting professional massages, using a hot tub or a sauna, and using early cue detection to prevent it from returning. Also, see Chapter 11: Reduce Tension and Conserve Energy.

ACCEPTING HEALTHY EMOTIONS

There are times when our emotions run high and it's healthy. Although you might argue that it's natural and healthy to be frustrated after spilling coffee on your pants, I'm talking about more difficult situations, like grief. In the following situation it would be normal and healthy to feel emotion and you would not expect acceptance to free you from pain.

Let's say that you have a dog and you let him run around in the front yard because you have an electric fence. Imagine that someone comes speeding through your neighborhood, loses control of the car, and kills your dog. It's unlikely that you will just accept this situation and feel no emotion. In fact, if you did respond this way I would be very concerned that you are numb and have serious deeper emotional issues. It is likely that you will feel very sad about your dog and that you will feel anger toward the speeder. In this situation, it is best to accept your emotions, but expect that in these types of instances acceptance will not make your anger and sadness go away because these emotions are healthy.

If you do not accept the healthy anger and sadness, you will likely experience additional emotions that are unhealthy. By accepting your healthy emotions you can prevent unhealthy emotions from taking over. Your initial reactions are often healthy; it's the reactions to the emotions that are typically unhealthy.

If you are uncertain whether your emotions are healthy or not, think about what most people would feel. Would most people get angry and sad if a speeder killed their dog? Of course they would. Regardless of whether or not the emotions are healthy, if you cannot accept the situation, accept your feelings about the situation. Often if we completely accept our emotions about a trying situation the unhealthy emotions will disappear and the remaining healthy emotions will persist in order to help us protect ourselves and allow healthy grief reactions. When we lose someone close, even the healthiest are likely to feel sadness. Fear and anger can often help us to protect ourselves. For more on the benefits of fear and anger see Chapter 5: Don't Worry, Problem Solve and Chapter 14: Assertiveness.

No matter what the situation, acceptance is helpful whether you are accepting the situation, accepting your emotions, or both. Once you have accepted your circumstances and emotions, it is often much easier to take action and, if warranted, work to change the situation.

Live It!

1. When feeling any uncomfortable emotion, observe it almost as if you're an outsider looking in. Notice where it's located, how much space it takes up, what it would look like if you could see it, and how it would feel if you could touch it. Accept it even though it's uncomfortable, much like a charley horse that is painful but causes no anxiety. Allow it to be there and resist any urge to try to push it away.

2. Use the optional recordings or scripts (found in this chapter) of emotional acceptance and observation of thoughts.

Chapter 9

Better-But-Believable Thinking

Worry is interest paid in advance on a debt that never comes due.
  - Derived from William Ralph Inge

Happiness is not so much a result of what life brings to you, as the perspective that you bring to life.

You have probably heard of cognitive therapy.[i] It is a systematic method of changing the bad habits of thinking negatively to new, healthier ways of thinking. The goal is for individuals to develop a more positive outlook on life that results in less anxiety and depression, as well as to

---

[i] *The most popular book on cognitive therapy is* <u>Feeling Good</u> *by a psychiatrist named David Burns. However, psychologists Aaron Beck and Albert Ellis preceded Burns in developing the concept.*

reduce other uncomfortable emotions that can occur as a result of negative thinking, such as frustration and guilt.

Do not confuse cognitive therapy with positive thinking. If positive thinking alone worked really well for you, you probably wouldn't be reading this book. Just about everyone tries to think more positively at some point in life, but it usually doesn't work very well. The main reason it doesn't work is that positive thoughts make you feel better only when you believe them. When in a stressful situation, people tend to reach for the most positive thought, rather than a believable and moderately more positive alternative to their negative thinking. Because most people don't believe the Pollyanna thoughts, they don't feel better from thinking them. Deep down inside they know them to be untrue; consequently, they easily give up on trying to change their habits of thinking negatively.

One way to look at it is to remember that cognitive therapy is not about putting on rose-colored glasses. Rather, it is about taking off the "poop-colored" glasses and putting on clear prescription glasses to see things as they are. While wearing the clear glasses, try to have no expectations at all. That way you will not be disappointed, but you will not be feeling stressed and depressed either. While wearing the clear glasses, however, it is best to avoid focusing on negative things unless you can use problem solving to help prevent unwanted outcomes. Once you have done your problem solving, refocus on the whole picture with greater emphasis on the positive side of reality.

For example, let's say that you are worried about a meeting with your boss tomorrow in which you're planning to ask for a raise. You've done the problem solving, you know what you want to say to him, and you are still worried about it. You realize that you are thinking, "He's going to turn me down and give me reasons why I don't deserve it." In a feeble attempt to stop worrying you might try to think more positively, forcing the thought: "I'm sure it will go well and I'll get that raise." But the reality is that you are not sure you will get a raise; otherwise you wouldn't be worrying about it. That thought is completely useless because you don't really believe it. If you have any evidence that it might not go well, you won't buy that positive thought and therefore it will not be helpful. The feelings of fear will linger.

A much more helpful alternative is to tell yourself, "I think I deserve a raise and my boss might think the same." Another one is, "There is a chance that I will get a raise and I've got my game plan." Finally, a third, but certainly not the only other possible group of thoughts is, "Worrying about it now isn't going to change the outcome. I'll probably know by tomorrow afternoon, so no need to engage in fortune telling now." These thoughts are all more helpful because they are more accurate than thinking that you will definitely get the raise and less distressing than worrying that you won't get the raise at all.

Other cognitive therapists have concentrated on elaborate systems of identifying types of thoughts, such as "shoulding," "catastrophizing," and "mindreading," just to name a few. Then they give specific suggestions on how to counter each type of thought. While it is often helpful to objectify these types of thoughts and get specific suggestions on how to deal with them, it can also get cumbersome. The result is that the laborious process can sometimes increase stress, or the time commitment involved can cause a person to abandon his or her efforts.

SIMPLIFYING COGNITIVE THERAPY

Tom Borkovec simplified cognitive therapy for worriers into a Socratic approach to it. He suggested that worriers ask themselves: "What is something equally true or *more* true that is less anxiety producing?" The idea is that most worries are very negative, they often reflect the worst-case scenario, and there is almost always a thought that is more positive, less anxiety producing, and yet true.

Given that stress often involves something that is anger producing, frustrating, or irritating and not just anxiety producing, one could substitute any of these phrases for the phrase *anxiety producing*. For example, when you are frustrated you could ask yourself, "What is something equally true or more true that is less frustrating?"

Although much simpler than the aforementioned symptoms, some people *still* find the phrase, "what is something equally true or more true, but less _____," cumbersome. Therefore, I have simplified this concept even further. The new Socratic question to ask yourself when you are feeling stressed is, "What is better-but-believable?" or for short, "B³": **B**etter-**B**ut-**B**elievable.

PRACTICING B³S

The example I like to use to illustrate B³s in action is that of a mother who is stressed about her son asking if he can ride his bike with some friends. She is worried he will get hurt or even killed riding his bike. Her stressful thought is, "I don't want him to ride his bike, because I am so afraid he's going to get hurt, or even worse, be maimed, paralyzed, or killed."

In this situation, thinking the most positive thought of "I'm sure he'll be fine" will not work, because it is not believable. Her fear is based on the reality that children get hurt on their bikes every day and in rare instances, the results are tragic. She knows that he could get hurt, and she may find herself reflecting on experiences in which she, her son, or someone close to her was hurt in an accident, even if it wasn't on a bike. However, the reality is also that he is very unlikely to get hurt that day and very likely to be safe. In addition, most of the time kids get hurt on their bikes it is an injury from which they will completely recover, such as a skinned knee. Nonetheless, fear is fueled by the fact that there is never a guarantee of safety. However, barring problem solving, which has limited applications in this case, the mother's focusing on this fear is not only useless but also causes a lot of undue stress.

Before you read on, I'd like for you to jot down three to five B³s that might help this woman to feel less stressed and less worried. If you have a pen or pencil handy, do that on the following page now. Otherwise, make a mental list.

1.

2.

3.

4.

5.

Are all of your B³s related to safety? If so, try to think outside the box. Try to come up with at least two thoughts that are better than "what if he gets hurt" but that are not about safety.

Okay, now take a look at my list.

1. I cannot protect him from everything; I could keep him inside and he could get hurt in here too.

2. Millions of kids ride their bikes safely every day.

3. Millions of people ride their bikes safely throughout their lifetime.

4. There is at least a 95 percent chance that he will be fine.

5. If he does get hurt, it will likely be something from which he will recover, like a skinned, bruised knee.

6. Getting skinned up and bruised is part of being a child. It's to be expected from time to time.

7. If he does skin his knee or elbow, he might be a little more careful in the future.

8. He's wearing a helmet.

9. There is safety in numbers.

10. I complain that he plays video games too much; this is good that he's getting exercise.

11. He will socialize and bond with his friends.

12. If I don't let him go, his friends might make fun of him or at the very least he'll feel less a part of the group.

13. He will be angry and sad if I don't let him go. While I know that it's wrong to allow him to do things because he will be angry with me, I know that I tend to be overprotective and it would be unreasonable for me to ask him not to ride his bike, a normal activity that boys his age do.

14. If I don't let him go, he'll ask why. When I tell him that I'm afraid he'll get hurt, he might become overly fearful, or worse, he may retaliate and take bigger risks.

15. He will probably have a lot more fun riding bikes than whatever else he'd do.

16. He will get a chance to improve his gross motor skills.
17. Those motor skills can help him to improve his confidence in sports, and that is likely to transfer to other parts of his life.
18. Getting exercise is great for his physical health.
19. Getting exercise helps his emotional health as well.
20. He'll probably be more relaxed this evening because of the exercise.
21. He'll burn less electricity than if he stayed home and played video games.
22. He won't mess up the house while he's outside riding his bike.

Notice that less than half of the thoughts listed here are about safety. I mentioned the positive qualities of socializing, getting exercise, having fun, and improving his motor skills and thereby improving his confidence. I also recognized that he would be justifiably angry and sad if she tried to stop him. In addition, I thought about him becoming fearful about riding his bike as well as the possibility that he could retaliate by taking more risks to try to prove to her that she can't control him. I considered how good things can come out of "bad" things such that if he sustained a minor injury it may result in his being more careful, thereby helping to prevent something catastrophic. Finally, I considered the advantage that he can't mess up the house while riding his bike.

A common mistake while learning cognitive therapy is to continue to focus on the negative in the construction of the more positive thought. So if you wrote or thought, "It is highly unlikely that he will get seriously hurt," or "There is less than a 1 percent chance that he will sustain a serious injury," you are still focusing on the possibility of him getting hurt. You might even start to visualize him in the emergency room. On the contrary, if you think that there is a better than 95 percent chance that he will be safe, you may visualize him coming back unscathed and with a smile on his face. In fact, visualizing the positive, realistic thought can be very helpful, particularly if you find yourself visualizing the negative outcome.

Try this exercise. Pretend that you are in this situation and you are afraid that your son (even if you don't have a young son) will get hurt or killed on his bike. Say this out loud if you are somewhere private, or just think it and feel it: "There is greater than a 95 percent chance that he will ride safely." Notice how this feels. Now say, "There is less than a 5 percent chance that he will get hurt." Most people report that the former feels better. So when you do your B^3s, word them in a positive manner.

Now it's time to try cognitive therapy and B^3s for something that is directly relevant for *you*. Think of something that has been pressing on you and stressing you out. Write it down here:

Now think of as many B^3s as you can for this situation. If you are having difficulty, have a friend, colleague, or family member help you. Worriers tend to be inflexible thinkers, so if you consider yourself to be a worrier and can't come up with ten alternative thoughts, or none of the thoughts are helpful, consult with someone who isn't a worrier. But try to come up with as many as you can on your own before you ask someone else to help.

1.

2.

3.

4.

5.

6.

7.

8.

9.

10.

In the margins next to each B^3 that you have written, rate the thought on a scale from 1 to 10 on how helpful it is, with 1 being not helpful and 10 being very helpful. Again, if you are somewhere that it is appropriate, say each statement out loud.

Now circle one to three of the thoughts with the highest ratings. If you have several that are rated the same, decide which ones are most helpful. It's usually best to limit your choices to three; however, if there are additional choices that help in a different way, include them. Say these statements aloud.

Rewrite the one to three B^3s that you have chosen on a small piece of paper or large sticky note so that you can refer to them later. When this worry re-emerges, pull out your statements and, if you can, say them aloud; otherwise reading them to yourself will be calming.

Better yet, memorize these calming thoughts. Be sure to really feel these thoughts rather than robotically reciting them. When applicable, visualize them as well (e.g., with the above example, visualize your son coming home with a big smile on his face).

Remember, too, that sometimes these alternative statements and problem-solving statements are one and the same. In other words, sometimes a problem-solving statement like "I'll make sure he is wearing a helmet" is a B^3 as well. These are often the best alternative thoughts because you are exercising some control and often improving the outcome. At least you will probably reduce your stress, while having a more positive perspective.

In many cases you will not feel motivated to create a long list of B^3s, rate them, and choose the best ones. As an alternative, when you are feeling stressed, identify the thoughts that are behind these feelings and replace them with B^3 thoughts. Consider that if you think one negative thought and follow it by one B^3 thought, the negative one is likely to "win out." This is because your long-lived habit is stronger than the new habit you are trying to

> ## Nip It in the Bud
>
> Do you have any nervous habits, such as biting your nails, tapping your foot, or drumming your fingers? If so, this is a good reminder that you are beginning to get stressed out and it's time to apply mindfulness, let go of tension, or apply another relaxation technique. If these strategies are not helpful, assess what thoughts you are having that may be creating your tension and find a B^3 that helps soothe this stress. Remember to periodically change the color of the sticky notes you are using to remind you to catch your stress early. Consider writing a key word to one of your B^3s or the whole statement on some of these sticky notes.

develop. Therefore, when you catch yourself thinking a negative thought, try to think of at least three B^3 thoughts. Not only will thinking three B^3s help to overshadow the negative thought, but also you'll be more likely to come up with one that is really helpful. Again, if you can say them aloud, do it. If this doesn't do the trick, go back to the problem-solving exercises from pages 51-53 and consider getting input from someone.

BEYOND B³S

In addition to changing your thoughts directly by thinking of B^3s, there are certain questions you can answer that may help to put your worries in perspective. For instance, how often does the thing that you are stressed out about turn out better than you had feared? When this happens, to what degree did your worrying help to make things turn out better? Or phrased a little differently, are you glad that you worried? For example, in the above scenario, if your son did get hurt on his bike would you be glad that you worried about him riding?

If you are like most worriers, you look back and think about how you stressed out for little or no reason. You might think back and recognize that there was a reasonable cause for concern, but that the majority of your thoughts were worries. Worries can create a false sense of control, but they are bad habits that don't include an effort to solve potential problems or maximize the outcome [see Chapter 5].

— Here are some other questions to consider regarding things you worried about recently that are now in the past:

1. Do you think things would have turned out worse if you had not worried? If so, was the stress worth it?

2. If you think your anxiety did make a difference, how much of it did you really need in order to make things turn out okay?

3. Could you have problem-solved more effectively with less worry?

4. Could you have used alternative statements to feel better?

5. Did worrying make the outcome worse?

6. How much does the event really matter now?

And here are some questions to consider for things you are worried about now:

1. Will this matter a week from now? A month from now? A year from now?

2. What are the advantages to worrying about this?

3. Am I confusing reality with my mythical fears and emotions?

4. Am I exaggerating the likelihood that the worst thing will happen?

5. What is the best thing that could happen?

6. If children being murdered is a 10 on the awfulness scale, what rating on the awfulness scale will this be at the worst?

7. If the worst occurs, what good might come of it?

8. What are some situations in which things seemed to be really awful at the time, but ultimately good things came out of them?

When you have difficulty relaxing and letting go of worrisome thoughts, answer these questions and it will likely help you to put things in perspective.

Now that you have considered how frequently things turn out better than you had feared, think about the alternative. How often do the things that you worry about turn out as bad as or worse than you had feared? In these situations would they have turned out differently if you had worried more or less?

Think about something specific that you worried about recently that you have stopped worrying about only because the situation is now in the past. In this situation, would it have been better, worse, or about the same if you hadn't stressed out about it? Also, do you think that things would have turned out better if you had worried about it more than you did? Do you think that your worrying may have prevented you from considering creative solutions?

Avoid Words of Extreme

Be mindful of words and phrases of extremes, such as always, never, constantly, or every time. A characteristic of B^3 thoughts is incorporating more moderate words. Some examples include the use of usually instead of always, infrequently instead of never, frequently instead of constantly, and so forth. These words of moderation tend to be more accurate and generate less stress.

Also be mindful of "what if's." When you say these two words it is almost always followed by a catastrophic, or at least a very negative, thought. I encourage you to play "angel's advocate" such that after each catastrophic thought, you think of the best thing that could happen. Then think of a range of more positive outcomes that are possible. Finally, consider what is more likely, and of course consider whether there are measures you can take to make things better.

Now consider the effect of your beliefs on your behavior. If you think negative thoughts, you are likely to be less motivated. You are also likely to affect the way others perceive you. For instance, if you think that you probably won't get that raise, you will behave differently in the meeting with your boss than if you feel you can get it. In the days leading up to the meeting, you might cut corners or work below your potential. You might not smile at him when you see him in the hall and may communicate with him in a less confident manner.

In other words, you may create a self-fulfilling prophecy such that your negative thoughts lead to ineffective behaviors, which lead to the denial of the raise because your boss sees you in a more negative light. Conversely, if you think you have a good chance of getting the raise, you may hold your head high, appear confident, and be able to discuss your raise in a way that will help you to get it.

Let's say that you got fired from your job and you run into an acquaintance on the street. She asks how you are doing and you say: "Well, I got fired from my job and I'm pretty depressed about it. I'm looking for something, but I just don't see anything that I think I'd like. I'm worried I'm going to be unemployed forever." If she knows of a job possibility, she will probably be reluctant to tell you because she may not want to refer someone who is negative. Or you are so negative that it doesn't even cross her mind. She may also assume that if you don't see anything you like, you won't like the job that she knows about, so she doesn't bring it up.

In contrast, let's take that same scenario from a different angle. When the woman asks you how things are going, instead of being negative, what if you were to say: "Under the circumstances I'm doing really well. I lost my job and I'm looking for something. My last job wasn't a great fit, but it was good enough that I was willing to stick it out. So I'm looking at this as an opportunity to find something that suits me better." In this case, she'd be much more likely to refer you to a job she knows about or make some other useful suggestions about how to find a job.

Most worriers admit to two things. First, if the bad thing they had worried about happens, they agree that it probably would have happened even if they worried more about it. Second, if it doesn't happen, they agree that it's not their worrying that prevented it from happening. For instance, if someone were afraid that his or her son was going to get killed riding his motorcycle, I would ask the person, "If your son does get killed riding his motorcycle, are you going to be glad that you worried about it?" I would also ask, "Do you think that worrying about him more could have somehow prevented it from happening?" Most worriers would answer both of these questions with a "no." In summary, this line of questioning can help you to realize that worry is useless.

Live It!

1. When you are feeling stressed, be mindful of what the negative thoughts are in your mind. Come up with at least three B³s. If appropriate say the most helpful ones aloud two or three times.

2. For particularly tenacious negative thoughts, brainstorm a list of B³s and then consider getting input from others who are more positive. Choose one to three of the most helpful, and write them down or say them aloud. Memorize them or carry the list with you so that you can recite them when the negative thought recurs.

3. Use the list of questions on pages 113 - 114. Circle the ones that you find most helpful. Consider copying these pages or marking them.

CHAPTER 10

STOP "SHOULDING" ON YOURSELF

People who are under a lot of stress are often anxious because they place a lot of pressure on themselves. This is particularly true of perfectionists who come to my office because stress is interfering with their productivity. Frequently the pressure is excessive because they are thinking that they "need to" do this and they "should" do that. This habit can become so engrained that some people think or say the words "I need to," "I have to," or "I should" well over two hundred times a day. I know this because I have actually counted during the first portion of some psychotherapy sessions, to make a point of how pervasive these stress-inducing words occur in their communication. Albert Ellis refers to this nasty habit as "musterbation." The word *must* is something I heard my grandparents say, which is not as often used today. Nonetheless, "musterbation" is a pretty humorous name for this bad habit.

Learning to change this habit and relieving the pressure associated with "shoulding" on yourself is part of cognitive therapy. This is one habit of thinking that isn't as amenable to thinking better-but-believable thoughts. This is because it is a habit that is so engrained and occurs so frequently that without extra help identifying it, most people are unaware of the amount of stress that "shoulding" creates. Therefore, I am devoting a separate chapter to changing it.

"Shoulding" on Yourself

Notice the word shoulders has the word *should* in it. Think about when your shoulders are tense. Consider how much of that tension you can attribute to the "shoulds," "have to's," and "need to's" you think and say on a habitual basis. Although there are a few exceptions, most people learned this habit from their parents. "You need to clean your room" or "You have to go to sleep" are common refrains. As a child, the consequences might have been such that you really did *feel* like there was no choice. The fact is that in many of these situations you did have a choice. Even though the consequences you would face for not doing it might not be worth it, you still had the choice to not do it and suffer the consequences. Therefore, as an adult you *feel* as though you have no choice when you hear people tell you that you "should" do something or that you "need" to do something. However, the bigger problem is usually the self-imposed "shoulds" that you habitually tell yourself.

Again, you probably learned to feel these imperatives from the mouths of your parents. Even if they said it nicely, should and need are words that place a lot of pressure on an individual. If you didn't learn it from your parents, it may have been from older siblings, teachers, coaches, and other adults in your life who "needled" you or "shoulded" on you. You may have felt as though you were irresponsible or a bad person or a failure if you didn't do what they said that you needed to do. Therefore, you usually would do it to keep yourself from feeling guilty or like a failure. The result is that your habits were negatively reinforced. Negative reinforcement is when a bad or uncomfortable thing is removed; the relief from this change reinforces, or increases, that behavior. In other words, if you are relieved of guilt by giving into a "should" and that relief feels good, you will feel at least as guilty the next time, so chances are you will repeat the behavior to relieve the guilt. That is why it's so hard to stop being emotionally ruled by both self-imposed "shoulds" as well as "shoulds" from others.

What matters now is how you use these words today. Really about the only thing you absolutely need is to breathe, eat, sleep, and have shelter. But when we hear or think the word need we may feel as if dire consequences await us if we don't respond to the command. Many people use these imperatives as an unhealthy way to motivate themselves. You might mistakenly fear that without these words you will become a couch potato or end up living under a bridge. The truth is that most of the time these words are actually counterproductive. They add tension and pressure, sometimes interfere with concentration, detract from enjoyment, and often zap your energy.

An interesting observation I have made is that sometimes even the things that people enjoy end up on their to-do list, which creates stress when people feel that they need to do them. Even if something is usually fun, or at least pleasant, the individual may be feeling as though it's a task or a chore. Instead of looking forward to it they might feel weighed down by that one additional thing on their list.

Here is an example of a dialogue I might have with a client. We'll call her Jeannie.

> **Jeannie:** *I have so much to do. I have to go to the grocery store on the way home and then I need to call the electrician again because our lights are still flickering and then we have to go out to dinner tonight with some friends.*
>
> **Me:** *You **have** to go to dinner with these friends?*
>
> **Jeannie:** *Yeah, we already made the plans.*
>
> **Me:** *Are these people whom you don't like?*
>
> **Jeannie:** *Oh no, I like Brett and Mandy a lot. But I have to get dressed and ready and it would just be easier to stay at home.*
>
> **Me:** *So, you don't have a lot of energy to think of getting ready and going out and keeping up conversation and so forth.*
>
> **Jeannie:** *Yeah, at the end of the week I'm just so tired.*
>
> **Me:** *Could you find out if they are available tomorrow night instead?*

Jeannie: *Well, they have kids, so I'm sure they already have a baby-sitter and Saturdays aren't usually good for them because they go to church early on Sunday.*

Me: *Okay, so you've gone out with them on a Friday before.*

Jeannie: *Oh yeah, several times.*

Me: *How many times have you been sorry you went out with them and wished you would have stayed at home?*

Jeannie: *Well, you have a point there. Once I get out I usually have a really good time with them. But one time I fell asleep in the movie we saw because it was kind of slow and I am pretty tired on Fridays*

Me: *So, it sounds like you really do want to go and you will have fun and be glad.*

Jeannie: *Yeah!*

Me: *I'm wondering too if you could just refuse to see a movie on a Friday night and maybe even suggest a rush-hour show on a Saturday with dinner afterward? They can be back home early enough to get up for church and you will be more rested. It seems that they could be a little more flexible in the future. Do you agree?*

Jeannie: *Well, yeah, but they need to get up early for church.*

Me: *Is it more important that they're not tired for church than it is for you not to be tired when you're out with them?*

Jeannie: *Yeah, I see what you're saying, but they always vie for a Friday.*

Me: *But the truth is that you don't **have** to go out with them tonight and you don't **have** to go out with them any other Friday night.*

Jeannie: *No, I disagree. I do need to go out with them tonight because I made a commitment.*

Me: *I do think it's good to keep your commitments. But would you agree that you could cancel tonight and they would likely forgive you?*

Jeannie: *Well, yeah? But . . . (pause)*

Me: *I'm not suggesting that you cancel, because we already established that you will probably have fun, right?*

Jeannie: *Yeah!*

Me: *What is more accurate? Is it more accurate to say that you have to go tonight, or that you could cancel, but you want to go because you will probably have fun, you like to keep your commitments, and you will likely be glad that you went?*

Jeannie: *I guess I don't really have to go, but the better point is that I do want to. Yeah, that helps! Now I'm starting to look forward to it rather than seeing it as another chore.*

Me: *Great! Also, next time you go to make plans with Brett and Mandy, what if you were to explain to them that you get really tired on Fridays and think you would enjoy things more on Saturday and then suggest that you just make early plans on Saturday.*

Jeannie: *Hmmm. That might actually work.*

Me: *I'd like for you to try a little exercise. Okay?*

Jeannie: *Sure.*

Me: *Okay, say aloud, "I have to go out with Brett and Mandy tonight."*

Jeannie: *I have to go out with Brett and Mandy tonight.*

Me: *Now say aloud, "I want to go out with Brett and Mandy tonight."*

Jeannie: *I want to go out with Brett and Mandy tonight.*

Me: *Is that true?*

Jeannie: *Yes, it is!*

Me: *Which one feels better?*

Jeannie: *I feel like I have to, but more than that I really do want to. I think I'll also suggest an early Saturday next time.*

Me: *Fantastic! When you stop feeling like you "have to," you start to be more open to your options. Now let's talk about the other things that you mentioned that you have to do: call the electrician and go to the grocery store. Could you go to the grocery store tomorrow? And could you write yourself a note to call the electrician over the weekend or on Monday?*

Jeannie: *Oh, I hate going to the grocery store on a Saturday; it's so crowded.*

Me: *You want to go today because it isn't as crowded. You could go tomorrow, though. You could just pick up a few things and go next week. For about $10, you could pay for the grocery delivery service to avoid going altogether. Could your husband go?*

Jeannie: *He doesn't like to go, but you know the only things we really need are cereal and coffee, and I could get them at the convenience store and then I could relax for a few minutes before going out tonight.*

Me: *Okay, just be aware that you have options and when you are saying "need to" or "have to" or "should," consider to what extent it really is a "want to" or a "could."*

As you can see from this exchange, it is important to make an effort to be mindful of your "shoulds," "need to's," and "have to's." First ask yourself what the consequences will be if you don't do something. If you still think you need to do it, ask yourself how much flexibility you have in doing it. For instance, it is typically pretty true that you need to do laundry sometimes. However, there is some flexibility. You could do it tomorrow. You could drop it off at the cleaners and have them do it. Perhaps you could hire someone to do it. You could wait until the weekend. Even if all of your underwear is dirty, you could go without. Even if you don't want to go without, you could. If you really want to have clean underwear, you could even go buy new underwear. If you don't want to shop, or go to the cleaners, or wear dirty underwear, then you *do* want to do laundry because you *want* clean underwear.

Now consider something that you really don't like doing. I don't know anyone who likes to clean toilets. If your toilet isn't dirty, visualize for a moment that you have a dirty toilet that bothers you when you use it. Now say out loud, "I need to clean the toilet." Notice how you feel. Notice your motivation level to clean it.

Now visualize the toilet clean and say out loud, "I want the toilet to be clean." Notice the difference in how this feels. Also, notice whether your motivation changes. We are always more motivated to do something positive than to do something negative. You are going to be more motivated to have the toilets clean than you are to want to clean the toilets.

Sometimes the key is to find a reason you want to do something, even if it is only to get it crossed off your list. Make certain you believe the statement. For instance, "I want my toilets to be clean" is significantly more believable than "I want to clean my toilets." Again, say both of these statements aloud to see the difference in how you feel.

On the next page there is a worksheet I developed that you can use when you are stuck on a "need to" or a "should" that is causing you angst.

Worksheet for Reframing Shoulds:

What is the "should/need to" statement?
What will happen if I don't do it?
What is the "want to"?
When else could I do it or what are the alternatives?
What would make it more pleasant?
Will I be glad that I did it?
Reframed statement(s):

There will likely be times that you are feeling as though you "should" do something, but it is also a "could." Perhaps it is something you'd feel guilty about if you didn't do it, but you could choose not to do it. For instance, let's revisit Jeannie's situation and say that even though she really likes Brett and Mandy, she really doesn't enjoy going out on Friday night because she is too tired to enjoy herself by the end of the workweek. She realizes that she is going only because she doesn't want to disappoint them and really would much rather lie on the couch. She realizes that she would be sorry that she didn't go only because she would feel guilty. On the following page is an example of what her worksheet might look like if this were the case.

Now, I'm going to give you a personal example. I am not one of these fortunate people who looks forward to going to the gym. But instead of telling myself that I need to go, I think about how I am always glad that I did, afterwards. I remind myself that I want to feel that sense of well-being, that I usually rest better, and that I want to stay in good

Nip It in the Bud

Think about what you do frequently throughout the day. Think of a creative way in which you can use these events to let go of unneeded stress. For instance, let's say you check your messages a lot. Put your phone in a new place, change the ringtone, or put a colorful rubber band around it.

Practice mindfulness when you are waiting. Whether you're sitting at a red light, held captive in the waiting room at a doctor's office, waiting for your computer to boot up, or stuck in a line, focus on your senses.

Mandy's worksheet in the event she doesn't want to go out Friday night.

What is the "should/need to" statement? *We have to go out with Mandy and Brett tonight.*

What will happen if I don't do it? *If I say no it will be easier to stay home and the world won't come to a crashing end. Rick, Mandy, and Brett will all be disappointed. I will get to lie on the couch watching a movie and eating popcorn.*

What is the "want to"? *I want to go because I honor my commitments. I don't want to feel guilty.*

When else could I do it or what are the alternatives? *I could always come home early if I am too tired; that would be a compromise. I also could stay home the whole night and everyone would eventually get over it.*

What would make it more pleasant? *It will be more pleasant if I can get a nap in beforehand. I can remind myself that I do like these people. Talking to Rick about leaving early if I'm really tired may help me to relax and enjoy the evening even more.*

Will I be glad that I did it? *I probably will be glad that I kept my commitment.*

Reframed statement(s): *I really don't have to go. I am choosing to go after getting a nap, and I am leaving the option open to go home after dinner. I think all of this will help me to enjoy the evening.*

physical shape. Even though it is not something I particularly want to do, I really do want to experience the positive effects of working out. If I were to fill out the worksheet it might look like the example on the following page.

Work is a little bit trickier because there are things that we do need to do because we want to keep our jobs. However, there is some flexibility even with work: breaks, location of doing the work, discussing options with your boss, choice of procrastinating, etc. In Chapter 5, on problem solving, I used a deadline as an example. As you may recall, the alternatives mentioned were to get it done even if it wasn't done well and then go back if you had enough time. There are several other "coulds" here. Another one is, "I can try, and if I don't finish it, the world won't come to a crashing end if the project is a day late." You could also suggest to the boss that she tell the client that it's finished, but you believe they will get a better product if you can have an extra forty-eight hours. If you really think your company expects way too much, you might even think of it like this: "I could meet their unrealistic standards, but that just sets them up to continue to expect me to meet them and pile on more and more work. I can take my chances and see what happens." So, look at the worksheet question of "When else could I do it or what are the alternatives?" as a problem-solving opportunity as well as a way to change perspective on "shoulds" and "need to's."

You can even look at work in terms of the dirty toilet situation. You may want to meet that deadline about as much as you want to clean dirty toilets, but if

An example of what my worksheet might look like.

What is the "should/need to" statement?
I need to go to the gym.

What will happen if I don't do it? I won't feel as good, I might not rest as well, and I'll probably be sorry I didn't go.

What is the "want to"? I want to have that feeling of well-being after I work out and I want to stay toned and healthy. I sleep better and feel more relaxed when I go.

When else could I do it or what are the alternatives?
I could wait until tomorrow or I could go for a run after work instead. I could go for a walk on my lunch hour.

What would make it more pleasant?
I'll take my MP3 player and put some lemon in my water. Sometimes I see friends there and that makes it more fun.

Will I be glad that I did it? No doubt! I always am.

Reframed statement(s): Although I feel unmotivated to go to the gym, I want to keep in shape and I know I will feel better and be glad if I go. I love that sense of well-being I feel from exercising, so I do want to go because I want to feel that.

you look at why you do want to meet the deadline it can be helpful. Next time you feel the weight of a deadline, say out loud, "I need to meet that deadline," and then say, "I want to meet the deadline because I want to keep my job." You might substitute other reasons besides "keep my job" with reasons such as "get promoted," "have a sense of satisfaction," "get a bonus," "get a raise," or "be respected."

On a similar note, many people really like the work that they do, but sometimes they lose sight of that because they make their agenda a list of "shoulds" and "need to's." Try to not lose sight of the "want to's" in your career and the enjoyment that you can get out of your job if you reframe your attitude toward work. You can lose enjoyment of tasks by viewing them more as things that need to be done and less as something that you may intrinsically enjoy if you stopped pressuring yourself so much with the "shoulds." For more on this topic see Chapter 16: Finding Balance in an Unbalanced World.

To summarize, when you feel stressed because you are saying that you need to do something, ask yourself why you want to do it. If it's something that you really don't want to do, usually there is a "want" in there at some level. For example, you may not really want to do all of the work involved to meet that deadline. But you want to meet the deadline because you want to keep the job. Also, experiment with using "coulds" instead of "need to's." Replacing a "need to" with a "could" is not as positive as a "want to," but "could" does allow more freedom and flexibility than "need to." Hopefully, at the close of this chapter you "want to" start decreasing the "shoulds," "need to's," and "have to's" and replacing them with "coulds" and "want to's."

"SHOULDING" ON OTHERS

A lot of people who "should" on themselves also "should" on other people. Be mindful of when you use imperatives and judgments with other people. "He should . . . " or "She should . . . " or "You shouldn't . . . " Even worse is telling people they need to do something. Remember that everyone has different values and ethics. Just because they are different from yours doesn't always make them wrong. Also, ask yourself if there is anything you can do to control what others do in the situations in which you are tempted to judge them in this way. Finally, what are your options if the person doesn't do what you want him or her to do?

To prevent the anxiety about "shoulds" in your children, as a parent you may want to give your children choices. For example, when your kid's room is a mess you might typically say, "You need to clean your room." Instead, what if you were to say, "You may play, but only after you clean your room" or "If you don't clean your room, you can't play video games." Similarly, "If you come home after curfew, you will not be permitted to take the car next weekend." If you tell your children that they need to clean their rooms, you are actually mistaken. They will not die if they don't clean their rooms. The reality is that if they don't clean their rooms they will suffer a consequence. Similarly, be mindful of how you use these imperatives with your spouse, friends, colleagues, and others in your life.

Doing this with your children can also help you to realize that you too have a choice when you tell yourself that you need to do something or you should do something. It can help you to recognize the choices that you have and either recognize that you don't want to face the consequences or that sometimes the consequences are worth taking. In other words, if you decide not to do something, the consequences are less than the effort of doing whatever it is you are "shoulding" yourself or "needling" yourself about. When you *want to* do something, you have more focus and concentration and it's done much easier, allowing you to be more productive and have better balance.

"Musterbation" makes you blind to the alternatives.

Live It!

1. When you catch yourself saying or thinking "should,"
   "need to," or "have to," rephrase using "want to" or
   "could" instead. Even when it is something you don't
   really want to do, think about the fact that you
   want to cross it off your list.

2. Ask friends, co-workers, or family members to
   gently point out when you say "should," "need to," or
   "have to"; then rephrase using "want to" or "could"
   instead. Say it aloud.

3. For "shoulds" that are particularly troubling, copy the
   worksheet and complete it.

CHAPTER 11

REDUCE TENSION; CONSERVE ENERGY

Sometimes less is more.

It is very common for people who are stressed to complain of fatigue. Stress requires a great deal of energy. More often than not, stress involves fear, anxiety, anger, or a combination. The reason we experience fear and anger is to protect ourselves. When faced with stressful circumstances, whether it's fear, anxiety, anger, or frustration, our bodies react with a sympathetic nervous system response, otherwise known as the "fight or flight response." This response "gears up" our bodies to help us fight or run as a means of protecting ourselves against danger.

This physiological response occurs regardless of whether we are being faced with a physical threat or an emotional threat. Whether you experience a sympathetic nervous system response because you are being chased by a bear or because your job is an unhealthy place for you to work, your body will respond in a similar way. If our bodies were designed perfectly, emotional stressors would produce a different response than physical stressors. It would help us to appropriately change or avoid emotionally unhealthy situations without the excessive energy and physical discomfort that is ironically meant to protect us from danger. This chapter is about reducing that excess energy. The ultimate goal is to use only the energy that you really need to function.

If you were to be chased by a bear or an attacker, the feelings of anxiety you'd experience would be very adaptive and useful. In this type of situation the sympathetic nervous system response sets off a number of physiological reactions in your body to help you protect yourself. Your breathing increases to get more oxygen (energy) into your blood, your heart pumps faster to get more blood to your arms and legs, and tension in those muscles increases so you can fight better and run faster. Your pupils dilate to allow in more light so you can see more clearly, particularly in darker places. Even the sweat on your hands helps your fingerprints to grip better to climb or use a weapon. In summary, fear can actually protect us when the threat is a physical one.

Unfortunately, most of the time that you experience these physiological changes in your body they are in response to an emotional threat. In these situations in which you are not in physical danger, you feel wound up with no place to go. Your body is geared up and prepared for you to fight and run, but there is nobody there to physically fight and nowhere for you to run. The feelings are not only useless, they are also physically and emotionally detrimental, causing you discomfort and draining your energy.

On the one hand, sympathetic nervous system responses can be useful when you are in a place that is psychologically unhealthy. I have seen numerous people whose anxiety or anger was manifesting itself in their body as an indication that they needed to leave a relationship, leave a job, or find more balance in their lives. This is a reason that I sometimes discourage people with mild to moderate levels of depression, anger, and anxiety to take medication; it may help them to tolerate being in a situation that is unhealthy for them to be in and prevent them from making a healthy change. The uncomfortable feelings you have are often a warning response that can help to motivate you to change your situation. I'm sure you have heard someone say "*run* out of that relationship" or "*run* from that job." Sometimes your nervous system will make you feel like running when you need to leave a job, end a relationship, or make other changes in your life.

On the other hand, most of the time the tension and stress we carry in our bodies due to the sympathetic nervous system response is useless. More often than not our situations are healthy, but our emotional responses to the workload and schedule, for example, give us more muscle tension, stress, and worry than we need. Most of the people I see want to stay in their jobs and in their relationships, but their stress levels are out of control. Their sympathetic nervous systems are gearing them up to fight and run, when all they need to do is walk. I don't mean walk literally, but figuratively. That is, take a walking pace in accomplishing things in the peak zone. Instead we often have a running pace going on in our bodies when the physical demand for our work is to sit and talk, sit and work on the computer, engage in meetings, drive, engage in a disagreement, and so forth.

To summarize, when you are feeling stress in your body, first identify the stressor (i.e., the situation that is causing you stress). Then decide whether it is best to change the stressor (e.g., leave your job) or change your reaction to the stressor (apply the strategies in this book). To change the stressor, refer to Chapter 5 on problem solving or consider seeing a career counselor, a personal coach, or a couples therapist.

Our excessive reactions to ordinary daily stressors cause most of us to use more energy than we need. It may be by breathing too fast or by carrying that uncomfortable feeling in our chests. We may also feel discomfort in our gastrointestinal systems. One of the most common reactions to stress is excess muscle tension from our bodies preparing us to fight and run. Our muscles run throughout the entire body. Therefore, excess muscle tension can cause a lot of discomfort and be a big drain on energy. Most people use more tension than they need to perform any given task, whether it's a very intense physical task or something as easy on the body as reading a book or watching TV. For example, right now, at this moment, ask yourself this question: "Do I need all of this tension to read this book?" See if you can let go of the excess tension in your body.

Now notice where your body is touching the surfaces beneath you - the chair, couch, bench, or bed, and the floor or ground. If you are lying on a surface, remain there. But if you are sitting and have your legs crossed, gently uncross them so that both feet are firmly on the floor. Imagine now that the surfaces beneath you are like sponges, but instead of absorbing liquid they are absorbing tension out of your body. Feel the tension draining into these sponges and allow gravity to help drain your muscles, freeing them of excess tension.

This exercise can be very useful while sitting in traffic, in a meeting, or in a waiting room. You can even use it while standing. When standing, exaggerate the imagined effect of gravity and allow excess tension to drain out of your feet. In any situation whether it is stressful or not, just asking the question "Do I need all of this energy?" or "Do I need all of this tension?" - followed by a quick body scan - can relieve a great deal of tension. As an alternative you can ask, "What's the least amount of tension (or energy) I can use and still _____?" In the blank insert your activity: "read this book," "drive this car," "sit in this meeting," and so on.

We have muscles from our head down to our toes, covering virtually every part of the body. Therefore, persistent muscle tension can cause a lot of discomfort and a lot of fatigue. In fact, not too long ago I received an e-mail from a woman whom I had treated more than ten years earlier. She had been diagnosed with chronic fatigue syndrome. I taught her a technique called progressive muscle relaxation. This procedure teaches you to detect when your body is getting tense and how to readily release this tension. Subsequent discussions about letting go of tension in order to conserve energy numerous times throughout the day proved to be very helpful. In her e-mail this woman thanked me and let me know that she had maintained her ability to function successfully in a pretty demanding career and as a mother. She attributed her success to learning progressive relaxation and to using the least amount of tension to get through her day. While there are no guarantees, learning to keep your muscles relaxed throughout the day is likely to help you conserve some energy and limit the amount of fatigue that you experience.

If you've had your sticky notes up for more than a week, I suggest that you change them to a different color. For the next week or two use the new sticky notes as reminders to gently let go of any excess tension in your body. If you're unable to release the tension, try stretching or tensing the affected muscles for five to ten seconds and then allow them to release. We can actually relax our muscles more effectively if we tense them first. It's like giving the muscles a running start to relaxation.

In time your goal is to be able to notice when your body is beginning to tense up and automatically release the extra energy. When you see sticky notes or other reminders, the goal is to be able to instinctively release unnecessary tension without having to think about it.

If you'd like to take this a step further, you may find progressive muscle relaxation very helpful. It's a very involved procedure, however, and is beyond the scope of this book as it requires several minutes of quiet, not active, relaxation. Developed in

Nip It in the Bud

Anytime you hear that your phone is ringing, you have a message, or you just got an e-mail, let go of any tension that you do not need; use the least amount of energy to continue your task.

the 1920's by physiologist Edmund Jacobson, it involves tensing and relaxing several different muscle groups in the body. Jacobson's technique takes about two hours. Fortunately, Bernstein and Borkovec revised the procedure and wrote a book that starts with a procedure that takes only about twenty or thirty minutes to get deeply relaxed. They use a step-down approach, such that as you learn the skill of deep relaxation you can gradually reduce the time involved by simplifying the process. Practicing progressive muscle relaxation à la Bernstein and Borkovec daily for two weeks leads to improved sleep, significant decreases in blood pressure if it is high (not if it's low), a decrease or elimination of tension headaches, decreases in chronic pain, decreases in

Tin Man to Scarecrow

To rapidly relax your whole body, try the Tin Man to Scarecrow strategy. To do this, first I'll ask you to tense all of the muscles in your body like the rigid tin construction of the Tin Man for about ten seconds. Then I'll ask you to let all of your muscles relax by thinking of feeling like the Scarecrow. Instead of tensing as hard as you can "like steel," tense your muscles between 50 percent and 75 percent of maximum tension, thinking of tin.

If you are in a public place where it's not appropriate to tense all of your muscles, think of your muscles as feeling "Tin Man like" for several seconds, or lightly tense everything except your face. Before you start, note that this should never cause pain. Ease into it and back off if you feel pain.

Tense like the Tin Man now and hold it for about ten seconds. Release like a Scarecrow: loose and light with no joints. Repeat if you wish.

irritability and anger, improved sexual satisfaction, and just a general increase in the subjective feelings of relaxation.

If you have a desk job and have a lot of muscle tension, I would suggest an ergonomics assessment. Without proper ergonomics, it may be difficult to let go of excess tension. Many companies will actually pay for an ergonomics assessment if you get a doctor's recommendation. Basically, an ergonomics assessment helps to position your hands and arms, your chair, and your computer keyboard in a way that minimizes distress on your body. One guideline is that your hands remain below your elbows so that you are taking advantage of and not fighting gravity as you write or type. Another guideline is that your upper legs are parallel with the floor and that your feet are flat on the floor. So if you are not eligible to get a free ergonomics assessment and cannot afford one, see to it that your feet are firmly on the floor, your knees are bent at a 90-degree angle with your upper legs parallel to the ground, and that your forearms are at least slightly below your elbows when typing. It is also a good idea to relieve your spine by standing and stretching, even briefly, at least every hour.

Live It!

1. Change your current reminders. For example, change your sticky notes to another color or change your ring tone. When you see or hear the new reminders think about letting go of any tension that is not needed. You may choose to write "loose" on your stickies or draw a downward arrow on them to indicate decreasing tension. The eventual goal is to automatically release the tension without having to think any words at all.

2. Once or twice a day, or more if you wish, practice Tin Man to Scarecrow by tensing all of the muscles in your body and then allowing them to completely loosen.

3. Consider (a) learning progressive muscle relaxation and (b) getting an ergonomics assessment of your work space.

Chapter 12

No Putzing!

How often does an evening or a weekend day go by and you think: "Geez! I didn't get anything accomplished today, I didn't do anything fun, and I don't feel like I really relaxed"? How is it possible that an entire day can go by and you accomplish little or nothing and yet didn't get enjoyment out of the day?

I call this phenomenon "putzing." Don't confuse putzing with futzing. The definition of futzing is "spending time aimlessly, lazily, or frivolously." Unlike putzing, futzing can be very healthy. While it's generally not good to be aimless, what would life be like if we never spent a Sunday afternoon lazily? Likewise, isn't life much better with occasional frivolity in it?

One definition of a putz is "a fool" or "an idiot." While a person who putzes is not necessarily a fool, it is a foolish *act* to putz. Putzing, as I define it, is lacking commitment either to enjoy time, or to be productive, such that time is spent aimlessly without relaxing, having fun, or being productive.

Putzing is most likely to occur when you really want to play or relax, but you feel like you "should" be productive. When this happens and you never really commit to either recharging your batteries or being productive, you are putzing. Putzing can be lying on the couch watching TV, being with a friend, taking a walk, or any number of leisurely activities, but having pangs of guilt about not working at the same time. Physically you're engaged in the leisurely activity, but emotionally you're feeling guilty and thinking about your to-do list. Instead of being in the moment and enjoying the activity, you are thinking something like this: "I should be working on the proposal, I need to put the dishes away, I have so many things to accomplish, but I don't feel like it. I'll do it later."

Putzing can also occur when you are making a greater effort to be productive, but you just aren't into it. It could be studying for a test, writing a proposal, doing accounting, or any other type of work. You aren't focused, move slowly, or otherwise are minimally productive. You can also putz when doing a job like cleaning the kitchen. You clean a bit, but you're unmotivated so you move slowly. For example, you may get distracted and read some junk mail that you find lying on the counter. Something in the junk mail reminds you of a friend, so you call her. You talk on the phone for several minutes or even an hour to avoid cleaning, even though there are many other things you'd rather be doing than talking on the phone. You didn't really enjoy the conversation and you got almost nothing accomplished.

Finally, another form of putzing is when you're trying to work while engaging in something relaxing. You really don't want to work but feel like you should, so you decide to watch TV while working at the computer or engaging in another work activity that requires cognitive energy. You don't enjoy the TV and you don't make much headway on your work either. There are a few exceptions to working productively while engaged in an enjoyable activity. These typically include activities that don't require a lot of thought. One such exception is folding laundry while listening to the radio, watching a movie or TV, or talking on a hands-free set. Bottom line is if you aren't really enjoying the TV, movie, or music or you are significantly slowed in your productivity, you are probably putzing.

Figure 5 might indicate the mind-set of someone who is lying on the couch watching TV, but thinking about work. When in a situation like this, you essentially have three options. One is to continue putzing. Two is to work. Three is to do something enjoyable (play or relax). What works best is to choose work or play, but at the same time plan to do the other later. Usually a little self-talk is helpful.

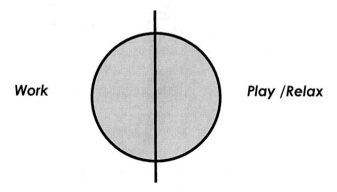

Figure 5. Mind-set while putzing.

To illustrate how to do this effectively, let's say that there is an individual named Michelle. She is watching TV on a Saturday but thinking about her to-do list for the day. She's watching TV, but she's thinking, "I should do the laundry; I need to look for a new job; I've got to start cleaning this filthy house. I have so much to do, but I don't feel like it. Ugh!" She's not really enjoying the TV show, because she's concentrating on the work she feels she "should" be doing, instead of really watching the show she isn't particularly interested in anyway. What's more, she's racked with guilt about not getting to her list. However, she can't find the motivation to get going because she's feeling the weight of doing all of these tasks and really wants to avoid them. I've heard some people say it actually makes them sleepy to think of their to-do list.

To control putzing, Michelle might ask herself, "Is this a program I really want to see or am I just avoiding work?" At this point she might even try the "should" worksheet from Chapter 9 because she's thinking "I should work; I shouldn't be relaxing because I have too much to do." If she's just avoiding work, she might consider what she really wants more, to get something

Stop Dicking Around

The Yiddish definition for the word putz is an obscene name for a penis. Have you heard the phrase "dicking around"? Young people often use this slang to mean wasting time. Putzing is a bit more polite way of saying the same thing. Depending upon your age and your personality, it may be more helpful for you to think of avoiding "dicking around" than to think of avoiding putzing.

accomplished or to relax and have fun. Perhaps she decides that she has worked really hard this whole week and she really wants some rest and relaxation, but watching this TV program is not how she wants to spend her time. Therefore, she decides that she'd rather walk to the coffee shop and read a novel she has not been finding much time to read. In order to really relax she reminds herself that nothing she has on her list is urgent and that she will at some point come home for lunch and then reconsider work. Or it might even be useful if she makes a specific plan to work later - defining when she will start, what she will work on, and perhaps a specific goal she intends to accomplish. So, for example, she may look at her watch and see that it's 9:15 a.m. She decides that she will leave the coffee shop between 11:15 and 11:30 and then she will put a load of laundry in and work on her résumé thirty minutes, start a second load of laundry, and then take another break to have lunch.

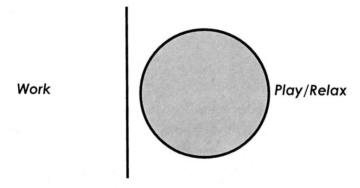

Figure 6. Michelle's mind-set at the coffee shop: committed to play and relaxation while recharging her batteries.

Once she makes this decision and gives herself permission to completely relax, she is able to enjoy the morning and at the same time recharge her batteries [Figure 6]. When she returns from the coffee shop she's more motivated and has some energy to work. She puts a load of laundry in and begins to look online for a new job with ease and focus. After lunch she is motivated to continue being productive.

Think about the difference between this scenario and the scenario in which Michelle continues to stay on the couch and watch TV just because she is avoiding work. She isn't interested in watching TV and even if she were, she'd be feeling too guilty to enjoy it. She's waiting to get motivated and continues to waste the morning away. Think about how little motivation she is going to feel when forcing herself to try to be productive that afternoon. If she putzed in front of the TV, guilt is much more likely to fuel efforts to try to work , rather than *wanting* to work because she feels re-energized. Therefore it is very likely that she will also putz in the afternoon while trying to accomplish something [see Figure 5]. She will be more likely to work slowly, be distracted, and lose concentration, while also feeling sluggish and disinterested.

In contrast, after fully relaxing and enjoying her walk, her novel, and her coffee, she will be much more likely to be productive and *not* putz in the afternoon. She'll be focused, motivated, and energized such that she will find the work less unpleasant and may even enjoy it.

We might say that putzing during play begets putzing during work. And on a much more positive note, the better we are able to completely let go of our responsibilities and enjoy our lives, the more we will get accomplished once we work. In addition to the benefit of having balance in our lives by being able to enjoy it, we recharge our batteries. Therefore, we can accomplish more when we do work. It's a win-win.

Nip It in the Bud

Remember to change the color of your sticky notes periodically. Take this one step further. Whatever the color of your notes at the moment, look for this color in your environment and when you notice that color, it too can be a reminder to use the strategies you have learned.

STOP feeling guilty for taking time off from responsibilities. Enjoy your life! Remember that there is no point in working if you can't enjoy your life. If you really can't enjoy yourself, but feel unmotivated to work, make a deal with yourself. For instance, it might be that you decide that you will put a load of laundry in and water the plants and then watch the movie for thirty or forty minutes, making a commitment to get some paperwork done in between folding the first load of laundry and the second load. Then finish the movie during and after the folding is finished.

If you are still having difficulty with guilt while relaxing, remind yourself that we all need a break from time to time. Even animals exhibit a post-reinforcement pause after finishing a task and getting the reward. That is, when animals work to get food, they pause to relax for

Pavlov's Dog and Putzing

Another reason it is not a good idea to work while watching TV, lying in bed, or being someplace where you often relax involves classical conditioning. Remember Pavlov's dog? Ivan Pavlov's initial focus of study was gastric function. When he was studying the saliva of dogs he noticed that the dogs salivated at the sight of meat. In addition, after some time passed the dogs began to salivate at the sight of the experimenter whom they associated with the meat even when that experimenter wasn't carrying the meat.

Humans are no different. People, places, smells, and things become associated with memories of feelings and behaviors in such a way that these stimuli (people, places, etc.) elicit similar feelings. So stimulus control means that there are stimuli in our environment that we associate with memory to the point that these stimuli affect our emotional and behavioral responses. This is why a Vietnam War veteran may find himself sweating and experiencing increased heart rate in response to hearing a helicopter or seeing Vietnamese people. He may even instinctively drop to the ground.

Stimulus control is also why it is not a good idea for you to work where you normally relax. For instance, if you work in the same place on the sofa where you typically watch TV, the sofa can become a stimulus for working. Therefore, when you sit there to watch TV you are likely to find yourself feeling less relaxed and will be more likely to be thinking about work instead of what you're watching. While I recommend that you not watch TV while working, if you insist on doing so, at least pick a different place to sit when you're working.

a bit before working again. Remind yourself that you may accomplish more if you let yourself play or relax.

This idea of not putzing relates back to the importance of taking breaks and productivity. Remember that you will accomplish more if your productivity quotient is 90 percent for four hours than if you work at 44 percent or less for eight hours. Another way to think about it is this: You will accomplish more in an hour in which you are 100 percent focused and productive than you will in two hours in which you are less than 50 percent focused and productive.

We are more motivated and productive if we've had some fun and relaxation. In addition, we can have more fun and more fully relax if we give ourselves full permission, without guilt, to engage in leisurely activity. Fully enjoying life's pleasures and being very efficient while working is the essence of balance.

Live It!

When you are aware that you are putzing, decide whether you would rather get something accomplished or whether you would rather relax and do something fun. Regardless of which you choose to do first, make a plan to do the other next (e.g., when I finish watching the movie I will wash the car and run errands - or vice versa). If you have difficulty deciding, do something productive for a short period of time (no more than thirty minutes) because it's always easier to commit to something small. Then it will be easier to enjoy yourself and will probably make it easier to continue to be productive.

Chapter 13

Procrastination: Not a Four-Letter Word

The word procrastination has always carried a negative connotation. Those who do it often continue their habit with guilt, even shame. Not only is it true that procrastination is not always a bad thing, but for some people procrastination can work very well. For these people, the worst thing about procrastination is typically the guilt about being a procrastinator and the nagging worry about it for days or weeks before getting started on the task.

If you are prone to worry about procrastinating, but do it anyway, you may be operating under the false assumption that if you put enough pressure on yourself and worry enough you might get started early. If you are continuing to do this, stop fooling yourself and face reality. If worrying hasn't led you to stop procrastinating in the past, it probably won't miraculously start now. Coming up with new and different strategies is the only way you can break your habit of procrastination. However, accepting your habit is another option for ending the useless worry about it.

Part of the reason that some people have difficulty kicking the habit of procrastination is that it often works. Even though they feel guilty, they are reinforced by the fact that they are typically more focused once they do finally get around to doing what they had been procrastinating doing. The experience of increased focus and improved efficiency when the pressure is on happens with many people and is a huge reason why people continue to do it despite feeling guilty and anxious about it while procrastinating. In other words, the benefits of procrastinating sometimes outweigh the guilt and anxiety.

This phenomenon of improved concentration when the pressure is on is particularly common among people who have attention-deficit hyperactivity disorder (ADHD). Contrary to the name of this disorder, people with ADHD actually have better attention than most when they are highly motivated. That is to say, Attention Inconsistency Disorder would be a more accurate name for this syndrome. Although they do have trouble concentrating sometimes, people with ADHD can concentrate and focus better than most people when they are highly motivated or very interested in what they are set on accomplishing. This is why procrastination can work extraordinarily well for individuals with ADHD. Having a short amount of time to complete a task can often trigger high motivation, thereby improving concentration and efficiency for tasks that would not bring much challenge or interest to the table otherwise.

Whether you have ADHD or not, you may want to evaluate the degree to which procrastination works for you. What are the benefits of procrastination and what are the disadvantages? If you procrastinate and it has caused you to miss deadlines, do poorly on exams, lose or harm friendships from failed promises, or get in trouble at work or lose your job - then you probably want to try to stop procrastinating and the second section of this chapter is for you. Otherwise, accepting that you procrastinate and making a minor tweak in your habits may be the solution.

In my clinical experience with treating procrastination, most people who have these issues are what I call "successful procrastinators." Their procrastination works because they almost always accomplish their tasks with few consequences other than a little bit of lost sleep, nagging from non-procrastinators, and perhaps unwarranted guilt and worry about the fact that they procrastinate. Successful procrastinators know on some level that these drawbacks are relatively minor compared to the advantage of the highly efficient work and the fact that their behavior routinely allows them much more time to do other things prior to engaging in the task.

Many people who procrastinate do so because when they work on something much earlier than is absolutely necessary they find themselves putzing or otherwise working inefficiently. One might call it "dawdling." You are working, but you are working more slowly and with less focus and attention because there is no pressure. You might allow yourself to be interrupted by phone calls; you may get a snack or attend to a detail in your work that is unnecessary and adds very little or nothing to your work. You might be working and wonder about something tangentially related to the subject matter, so you take the time to look it up online. In summary, people may procrastinate because if they didn't, they would be more easily distracted, work more slowly, work with less concentration, and overall just plain work less efficiently.

In contrast, once you have procrastinated and finally start to work, you are typically not tempted to dawdle or putz because you know that you can't. You either don't answer phone calls or wait to return them until you finish the project or really need a break. You work full steam ahead without being distracted by noises, impulses, or tangential ideas and unimportant questions. Your efficiency level is 90 percent or higher. Somehow you know that if you had started the project earlier, you would have put in twice the amount of time or more and yielded no better work. Or in some cases your work might be slightly better had you not procrastinated, but not at all worth the extra time you put into it.

PLANNED PROCRASTINATION

If you are a successful procrastinator with or without ADHD, I recommend something I call "planned procrastination." Planned procrastination involves two things: (1) acceptance, and (2) honest planning.

The first part is to accept that you are a procrastinator and that it works for you. You accept that the advantages of your focused efficiency outweigh the

Myth of Deep Breathing

You've probably heard "just take a deep breath." Most people interpret a deep breath as a big breath. Big breaths are unnatural and if you find them helpful it's probably only because they distract you from unwanted thoughts.

Taking a natural breath deep into the bottom of your lungs is much more efficient. This is because the only place that your lungs can absorb oxygen is deep into the bottom of your lungs. This is called diaphragmatic breathing because there is a muscle called the diaphragm that is attached to the bottom of your lungs. When you're breathing properly, this muscle contracts to allow the bottom of the lungs to expand, allowing oxygen to be absorbed into the blood stream.

Interestingly, people who complain of anxiety are much more likely to take shallow breaths from their chests. Bottom line, when you think of deep breathing, think of taking oxygen deep into the bottom of your lungs with a comfortable breath, rather than taking in a big breath. Watch a young child breathe and you will see their tummies expanding as they breathe in. Mimic the child's breath while they are at rest. Diaphragmatic breathing is another way to conserve energy.

lost sleep or other disadvantages such as anxiety, guilt, or frustrating your spouse or partner. And the good news is that planned procrastination is designed to help you decrease anxiety and guilt. In addition, you can share this chapter with loved ones who give you grief for procrastinating in hopes that they too can be more accepting of your habit, thereby decreasing your guilt.

The second part is to think about when you would ordinarily start working on a project. Be honest with yourself and think about when under typical circumstances, you would start to work on this task. Once you decide the date and time you would probably start, enter it in your PDA, Outlook, phone, or planner. This part of writing it down in your schedule is essential. When you write it down and plan it, then you are more likely to be able to let go of any worries and guilt about procrastinating because you have written down the time you are going to start. It's then easier to put it out of your mind. Again, be honest with yourself regarding when you would typically start. If you write down a much earlier time than you would typically start, it probably won't work. You'll probably still start as late as you would have and then will feel guilty and anxious until you finally start. However, if you write down a time just a little before the time you would usually start, then you might start a little earlier, but if you don't then there will only be a small amount of time that you are feeling guilty about procrastinating.

Once you start working on the project, you will probably also feel less guilt about waiting until the last minute. When you start working on whatever it is that you had procrastinated doing, notice how focused and productive you are. Begin to really appreciate these advantages to your procrastination.

Even if you love the idea of planned procrastination, you may decide that you want to procrastinate less due to loss of sleep or some other disadvantages, such as missing events or irritating your spouse. Please read on. Maybe you'll decide to combine planned procrastination with some of the other strategies in the next section.

COMMITTING TO SMALL TASKS

Inch by inch, life is a cinch.
Yard by yard, it is really hard.

This, the second section of this chapter, is aimed at the individual who is not successful at procrastinating. This section can be helpful if you find that you have difficulty getting motivated. Whether you feel it is inertia for dull and boring tasks or whether it is because you're overwhelmed and just can't get started on your long to-do list or huge project, you probably tell yourself that you should do it. But you really don't want to do it. Despite feeling this pressure you continue to be unable to find the energy to get started. The best way to overcome this and get started is to find small doable tasks.

You will probably agree that when you feel as though you only have a few small things to do (say, four) it's easy to get motivated to accomplish those things. But when you have four big projects and thirty to forty little things on your plate, sometimes it's difficult to do anything. You get bogged down with an overwhelming sense of responsibility, and that results in inertia.

The key to overcoming this is to commit to smaller, easily accomplished pieces. Break down larger commitments. This can be done in two general ways. The first is to divide big projects into subtasks and maybe even tertiary tasks. The second way is to commit to a reasonable, specific amount of time to work on that task each day or week.

Even though it was much longer ago than I'd like to admit, I remember working on my thesis and dissertation when I was in graduate school. It was overwhelming. It was very difficult to get started on a project that was going to take more than a year and literally more than a thousand hours to complete.

To get motivated I divided it into several small, doable tasks. I started by looking at big chunks - for instance, "write the introduction." This big chunk involved doing a literature review resulting in finding twenty articles, reading those and taking notes or highlighting, then summarizing into a draft, getting feedback from my dissertation chair, and eventually finishing the introduction. I decided about when I'd like to finish the introduction as well as all of the other major tasks and wrote these dates in my planner. I wrote in these goals over the course of a few months up to the proposal meeting.

Before I started working on my dissertation I broke it down into a few major tasks. Then I broke the first major task into subtasks that could be accomplished in about a week and wrote them in my planner. Then at the beginning of each week I divided the weekly goal into six daily tasks. I wrote each task on Monday through Saturday of my planner. This method allowed me an extra day if I had underestimated the amount of time it would take or if I had an unusually busy week. It also allowed a day to break from my dissertation if the tasks went well.

In addition, I did make a commitment to my dissertation chair to have each of the milestones accomplished. It helps to have culpability to others to stay on track, especially with large projects. Make commitments to friends and relatives who support you in accomplishing your feats. Check in with them on a regular basis regarding progress and goals. This works particularly well if you have someone else who is trying to accomplish a goal or change a habit for whom you can also be of support.

I finished my dissertation before I left for my internship, something my chair had never seen done in more than six years of being a professor; others on my committee could only cite one or two out of hundreds who had accomplished this feat.

Now you may think, "Well, she's organized" or "She's never had a problem with procrastination." But the truth is that in undergraduate school my roommates and dorm mates teased me mercilessly about my procrastination because I was the worst. I often started large projects the night before they were due, typically working until 4:00 or 5:00 a.m., sometimes pulling all-nighters. (Although, procrastination usually worked for me and resulted in good grades, I knew on a large task like this, I needed a plan.) I'm also not at all

Nip It in the Bud

Let time be your reminder. Use both sight and sound. Anytime you hear a clock ticking, hear the clock chime in the town square or college campus, or hear the grandfather or coo-coo clock in your home, use it as a reminder. When you see a clock or go to purposefully check the time, use it as a reminder to take things one at a time or use any of your other Active Relaxation strategies. Put a sticky note on your clock or a small piece of one on your watch.

organized. If anything it was my history of poor organization and procrastination coupled with my desire to earn my Ph.D. that led me to solve my procrastination problem by breaking it down into easily managed tasks and creating my own smaller deadlines. If I can overcome procrastination, almost anyone can.

But how does writing a dissertation compare to the more common tasks we face each day? Here's an example that many of you can relate to: a messy house. If every room in your house is a mess, it is likely to feel overwhelming to think of cleaning it. You look around and lose any motivation you may have had because it is so overwhelming and it seems that any efforts would barely make a dent in it. Therefore you give up and continue to live in the mess.

In this case, it helps to start by picking one room that you feel would provide the greatest stress relief if it could be clean. Let's say it's the kitchen. That still might feel like an overwhelming task, but not nearly as daunting as cleaning your whole place. The next step is to pick one kitchen task that would be easy to accomplish, preferably something that would take less than fifteen minutes, maybe even less than ten. For instance, you could commit to throwing away all the trash. Or you may decide to put everything on the countertops and tables away. If you have a fair amount of motivation you may decide to do both. Once you finish this task you will have a sense of accomplishment, albeit relatively small.

At this point one of two things will happen. One thing that could happen after completing the small task is that you might feel unmotivated to do anything else. If this is the case, at least celebrate your small, but important, feat. You finally got started! Make a commitment to do the next task the next day, or if it's a weekend or day off, you might even commit to doing it later in the day.

The other thing that is likely to happen is that by accomplishing this task you will feel energized and you might think, "It would be pretty easy to clean off the countertops and they look so much better." In just a few minutes you have clean countertops. You might stop at this point and be proud of your accomplishment. Then again, you might think, "I may as well load the dishes in the sink into the dishwasher" or "I may as well do the dishes." If you get this far, the only thing left would be the floor, and that would be an easy task for the next day. Or if you have time and energy, you might just find yourself finishing the job.

As stated previously, an alternative to choosing a small task or subdividing tasks is just to spend a certain amount of time on each project. One year, my New Year's resolution was to straighten or clean my house for ten minutes each day. It's amazing how much better my house looks today because I have kept this commitment. Depending on your motivation level and the type of task, you might commit to only ten minutes, or you might commit to a couple of hours. Much like the subtasks, you might spend ten minutes cleaning your kitchen, for example, and then decide that you are on a roll and want to continue. At this point, you could set a goal for an additional ten minutes or you could just continue at will. I suggest setting a timer because it can help you to focus your attention on the tasks at hand. Do your best not to allow distractions from the phone, reading junk mail, or otherwise taking your attention off the task. Be fast and focused, but not rushed. Think of it as a game to see how much you can accomplish while being mindful and keeping your body relatively relaxed.

THE BEST OF BOTH STRATEGIES

A third option is to combine the two strategies of planned procrastination and setting aside small goals. Do this by setting a small goal and giving yourself a time limit to accomplish that goal. Think about how much you would typically be able to accomplish in those final moments. For instance, say you are a writer. Commit to writing a draft that is at least three pages in ninety minutes. Actually write down the time that you plan to finish this task and avoid doing the things that you would avoid doing if you were down to the final deadline. Think about how much you are able to accomplish when you are working diligently after having procrastinated. See if you can mimic the feeling and behaviors of working after having procrastinated by making a commitment to finish that goal on time.

Alternatively, think about how much time you want to commit to your project and think about what your goal is. For instance, you have a free hour, so you decide that you could write two pages of a draft in that period of time. When you are finished, consider doing something to reward yourself even if it is just relaxing for a few minutes.

Various Strategies to Get It Done

I've found that by simply timing yourself on tasks you tend to avoid because you don't like them, you realize how you overreact to the size of the task. For instance, most people are surprised by how little time it takes to unload the dishwasher or put away a basket of folded laundry if you're focused. Timing tasks can help to prevent dawdling as well.

Another strategy to combat procrastination is preparation. If you have been avoiding a task, set out the equipment and any required clothing ahead of time. For instance, I had been avoiding installing my programmable thermostat. So, I went to the basement, got the drill, a hammer, and a screwdriver and took the new thermostat out of that annoying hard plastic packaging. It probably only took about three minutes to do these few things. However, it accomplished two things. One, it eliminated those steps so that my task was now simpler, and two, seeing the tools and the opened thermostat in plain view made it easier for me to remember and harder for me to continue to procrastinate so I could "just do it."

An additional example of this strategy lies in the case of the aforementioned kitchen. Let's say that you had done everything except for the floor and had run out of time or energy to do it. At that point it would take you about a minute to get out the broom, dustpan, bucket, mop, and soap. Then the next day, it will be easier to keep on task.

This strategy works out particularly well for exercise too. Set out your clothes, shoes, socks, and anything else you will need for your exercise the night before and pack your gym bag. You can still procrastinate, but if you combine this with setting a small exercise goal it will be easier for you to get moving.

Finally, use the "just do it" slogan coined by Nike. To add a little boost to this often ineffective strategy, use your B^3 from Chapter 9. For instance, "I'll be glad when I've finished it," or "Once I get started it will be fine."

Live It!

1. If procrastination has worked for you in the past, each time you start to stress about something you're procrastinating, be honest with yourself on when you'll likely start it. Write the task down in your planner.

2. If you're overwhelmed by a task, break it down into doable, small tasks and plan to do one daily, or take a day or the weekend off.
    -OR-
3. Commit to a small amount of time to work on this task each day.

Chapter 14

Practice Assertiveness

Few things cause more stress than being at odds with a colleague or a friend. As you read this you can likely reflect back on at least a few instances in which you felt tension, a knot in your stomach, or maybe even lost sleep over a conflict you had with another person. Many people avoid trying to resolve a situation because they are afraid that their discussion will end badly. They may worry that they will say something they will regret or that the other person may misunderstand them and that the outcome will make things worse rather than better. They may decide not to say something rather than take a risk. An active way to relax is to be able to resolve conflicts by expressing your concerns in a way that respects your rights and feelings as well as respecting the rights and feelings of the person with whom you have a conflict.

Most people understand what it is to be passive and most also understand what it is to be aggressive. However, there is a lot of confusion about what it means to be assertive. Some people think assertiveness and aggressiveness are the same thing, but they are mistaken. In short, an assertive approach is more respectful of others than an aggressive approach. Finally, there is also a lot of confusion about what passive-aggressive means. Let's start with an explanation of these terms; it's essential to have an understanding of these differences in order to practice healthy assertion.

People who are passive put the rights, desires, and feelings of others first. They have difficulty saying "no" and are often taken advantage of as their feelings and desires are frequently dismissed. In contrast, when people are aggressive they are not usually taking others' feelings into account. They may be loud, demanding, or even physically destructive, and they often focus solely on their own feelings and desires. People who are passive-aggressive are mean, disrespectful, or hurtful in a passive or indirect way. The intent is to harm or hurt someone without being outwardly aggressive. The healthy alternative is assertiveness. When people are assertive they are respectful of their own rights and

Nip It in the Bud

When people have someone frustrating in their lives, I jokingly say, "Put a sticky note on the person's forehead." While you may be able to do this with a small child, anyone else is likely to take issue with such a suggestion. However, you can sometimes prevent allowing this person to frustrate you by using that person as a reminder to relax. Anytime you see this stress-inducing individual, get into the habit of letting go of the unnecessary tension you typically feel when seeing him or her.

feelings as well as those of the person or people to whom their assertion is being directed.

Take the example of Jill who gets up at 7:00 a.m. to go to work. Her neighbors Abby and Mark are playing their stereo loudly at 1:00 a.m. If Jill were passive she wouldn't say a word or do anything to show her frustration. Instead, she would lie awake until the stereo was finally turned off. If Jill were aggressive she might pound on the door and shout, "You need to turn off your stereo. It's late and you have no right to be blaring it in the middle of the night." Or she might threaten to call the police or pose another threat such as waking them tomorrow morning when she gets up. Passive-aggressive would be if Jill purposefully blasted her stereo at 7:00 a.m. or ignored her neighbors the next time she saw them. If Jill were assertive, however, she would knock on the door and say something like, "I have to be up at 7:00 and I can't sleep because the music is loud. I'd really appreciate it if it could be turned down."

Don't Shout! Whisper?

This is a nice little trick to use when you feel you aren't being heard, even if you feel like shouting. Try speaking very softly - almost in a whisper! It can de-escalate an intense conversation. Ironically, shouters are often tuned out while whisperers are tuned in. People have to listen much harder to someone who is whispering or speaking very softly. What is more, if you are feeling angry it can help you to lighten up your emotions too. More importantly, it's pretty difficult to continue to yell when someone is whispering. While there are no guarantees that the person will stop shouting, this technique works more often than not.

Assertive concerns or requests typically start with "I" or "my." This may seem like it's selfish, but the reality is that you are taking responsibility for your feelings and requests. For instance, if someone is repeatedly late you may want to say something like, "My time is important to me. I don't mind waiting for a few minutes; however, I get frustrated when I'm left waiting for twenty or thirty minutes." Notice that the content of this message is difficult to debate because you are sharing your "perspective and feelings" rather than making a judgment that is debatable. Imagine if you were routinely twenty or thirty minutes late and someone said that to you; it would be difficult to argue about and yet you weren't attacked or judged.

Imagine the difference between that and someone saying something aggressive like this: "You are always late and I'm really getting sick of it. You are so inconsiderate." If you were the late person you would likely feel hurt, embarrassed, and/or angry and would be more likely to respond defensively and think that the person is being too harsh. Consider even a moderately aggressive response: "You are frequently late and I'd really appreciate if you could make a better effort to be on time." That response is accurate and not at all unfair, but it is still a little more aggressive than the previous assertive example and likely to result in more tension.

While I encourage using assertive "I language," it's important to recognize that starting a statement with "I" or "my" doesn't necessarily ensure that it will be assertive. It could still be aggressive or passive. For instance, "I'm really getting frustrated with you. I always have to wait for you" is aggressive. Although it starts with "I'm" it still puts blame on "YOU." When possible, leave the word "you" out completely.

Being passive can be when you say nothing at all. However, sometimes people try to be assertive but are still pretty passive. Being passive can include unnecessary apologizing, using "uuhhhs" and "ummms" too much, putting yourself down, avoiding eye contact, or suggesting in any way that your request might not be reasonable. For example, "Umm, I know you're really busy and that it's really difficult to time things, but if it's not too much trouble, it would be, ummm, I'm sorry, I just don't like waiting too long."

The content of what we say is very important in learning to be assertive. However, nonverbal communication, what we say without words, can be passive, assertive, or aggressive too. Nonverbal communication includes voice tone, facial expressions, body posture, eye contact, proximity to the other person, and gestures. Sometimes nonverbal communication can convey passive, assertive, and aggressive messages that are so strong that they override what is said in words. For instance, someone could use all the right assertive words, but if he or she has an angry facial expression, moves in very close to the other person's face, shouts, or stares at the person while speaking, his or her behavior would still come across as aggressive. Similarly, if a person speaks softly and looks down, the receiver might find it too easy to deny the request being made even if the content is perfectly assertive. For assertive nonverbal communication to match the assertive content of the message, the individual must speak audibly and clearly without raising one's voice. Eye contact that is diverted every few seconds is assertive, as are facial expressions that match the content (e.g., raised eyebrows versus a scowl). The bottom line is that even if the content is perfect, voice tone, posture, and facial expressions are actually more important than the words we use.

There is a continuum on the passive to assertive to aggressive scale. Communication about a conflict does not usually fall squarely in one category or the other. For instance, picture Jill knocking on Abby and Mark's door, averting eye contact, and saying, "Ummm, I'm sorry to bother you, but if it wouldn't be too much trouble, do you think you could, umm, turn the stereo down a little, please?" That behavior would be pretty passive, but not as passive as saying nothing, so it is somewhat assertive. Likewise, if Jill knocked really hard on the door and had a very angry look on her face when saying perfectly assertive words, she would be considered on the aggressive side of assertive. If you aren't sure what level of assertion is appropriate, try assertive escalation. Start with somewhat

Broken Record Technique

Part of being assertive is turning down other people's requests. When you feel that another person is unable to "take no for an answer," or is unwilling to agree to disagree, use this technique. No matter how hard the person tries to change your mind by coming up with different arguments, respond with the same answer repeatedly. Some examples: "The answer is still no." "I'm sorry; I'm just not comfortable with it." "Let's agree to disagree." This will tire the persistent person more rapidly, while making it easier for you to defend yourself.

passive assertion. If you aren't happy with the response, you can become gradually more assertive and, in some situations, somewhat aggressive.

Remember, too, that the appropriate degree of assertion versus aggression often depends on the context. For instance, a discussion with a colleague that may be considered assertive if you are working as an accountant or a massage therapist may be interpreted as "wimpy" or passive if you are working in an auto plant or in construction. Similarly, an assertive response at the auto plant might be considered aggressive in a health spa. In addition, family dynamics affect your communication style. If you grew up in an aggressive environment, you may still need to be somewhat aggressive with your family in order to get what you want. However, the whispering technique just might work.

Utilize mindfulness while practicing assertion. Notice how you feel as you address someone with an assertive response. Be mindful of which words or parts of what you are saying, or are about to say, are uncomfortable. Try to determine why you feel the discomfort. Is it because you are saying something inappropriate? Is it because you are afraid of the response you'll get? Do you have performance anxiety? For fear and anxiety remember that the best way to overcome it is to face it. The more you practice being assertive while visualizing the other person there, the easier it will get. Moreover, use assertion in real life on a consistent basis and it will gradually become more comfortable.

A great mindfulness in assertion exercise is to practice what you are planning to say to someone before you talk to him or her. Close your eyes. Put yourself in the other person's position. Imagine that you are hearing the words you plan to say, rather than saying them. Notice if you feel the way that you want him or her to feel and whether you're hearing the message you want to convey. Adjust as necessary.

A similar exercise is to stand in front of a mirror. Look into your eyes and listen as much as you can while saying what you want to say. Focus on how you feel as the recipient of this information.

Finally, remember to not always expect to have your way when you are assertive. This may be because the person with whom you are speaking is insensitive or selfish, your request may be unreasonable by most people's standards, or it may be that you just disagree and have different perspectives. By being assertive, you often learn more about the person and his or her perspective. Maybe you won't get what you set out to get. However, you may gain an understanding or get information about the situation that you didn't previously have such that you feel better about the situation and the person. Either way you are likely to learn something. When you are assertive you are more likely to get what you want, but even when you don't you can feel good about respecting yourself and others equally.

Live It!

1. Start by practicing assertiveness with people who aren't very assertive or others whom you believe are more likely to accept your assertion (e.g., strangers).

2. Use "I" language.

3. When possible, before you assert yourself, practice your message by speaking aloud and imagining that you are the receiver of what you are saying. Consider using a mirror. Adjust as necessary.

Chapter 15

Let Lists Work for You

One purpose of this chapter is to help you set priorities and get things accomplished in a more efficient manner. The idea is to be able to accomplish the same amount that you're accomplishing now but more quickly, such that you have more time to do the things you want to do. Alternatively, you may use the extra time to get more accomplished. Perhaps you'll do a little of both.

Another purpose of this chapter is to help you get your to-do list out of your mind when you want to relax and have fun. This new way of making lists can help you to be in the moment so that you are less stressed while working. It can help you to let go of your list completely while you're enjoying yourself. A big part of this is learning to make lists in a better way than the old-fashioned long list of items being scratched off as you probably do now.

There are a few ways you can make lists. One is the old-fashioned hard-copy list on one big piece of paper where you scratch off items as you complete them. This is not the best way to make lists. First of all, it's difficult to stay in the moment when you see a long list of items. Second, it's too easy to lose this type of list among other papers. There are few less frustrating things than trying to get things accomplished and having to take extra time hunting down your list. In addition, it's difficult to prioritize and easy to miss important items while sifting through those scratched off and those left. The good news is there are alternative methods of list-making that eliminate these problems.

STICKY-NOTE LISTS

For several years before Stickies was ever used on the Mac [see iPhones, Computers, the Web - Oh My!, on the next page] I had been using hard copies of actual sticky notes. Many of my clients have found this to be helpful, and for some it has been life altering. In short, rather than writing your list on one piece of paper, my system involves writing each item on your list on an individual sticky note. This way of making lists has several advantages over the traditional list, all of which I will get to shortly.

It is fine if you prefer using your iPhone, Blackberry, or computer for organizing your lists. However, I think it's helpful to at try the hard copy version of this list system first. Overall there is greater flexibility and some advantage to the tactile nature of the "real" notes. This is also very helpful if you are trying to avoid getting sucked into e-mail, surfing the Net, playing games, or getting on Facebook.

What I'd like for you to do is purchase the small sticky notes typically packaged as page markers. Alternatively, a less expensive way is to take the larger notes and cut them into narrow strips such that there is a sticky portion on each piece. I'd also recommend this option if you'd like to get started now and the larger notes are all that you have.

iPhones, Computers, the Web - Oh My!

There are several computer programs for using lists that you can download from the Web, that you can use on the Web, or that are already part of your computer system. For the iPhone there is an application called "Things," which costs $9.99. (Users have given it 3.5 stars out of 5 possible). There are also less popular applications for the Blackberry that are more expensive. One of the computer-based programs is called Stickies. This program is preloaded on the Mac. However, you can also get a Windows version of this same program. Other programs include Nutshell and MoRun Sticker at morun.com. Morun.com offers a free thirty-day trial and may be most like the hard copy version that I will teach you in the next few pages.

Before you begin writing down the tasks you would like to accomplish, take some time to consider color-coding these tasks. For example, I suggest you use a different color for errands than for other tasks. If you'd like, you can use different colors for work and home as well. You could even go as far as using different colors for different types of tasks. You could also color-code according to priority (although separating the notes in groups according to priority might be better, particularly because priorities change over time). You could color-code according to type of task: household chores, computer-related tasks, tasks that you look forward to doing, etc. Include small tasks that you want to accomplish today as well as larger tasks that you may not get around to for several days. Make a long, large list of everything you hope to accomplish in the next week or two, or even the next month or two, putting a different task on each sticky.

Consider dividing larger tasks into subtasks. For instance, if you are planning on cleaning out the basement, you might divide it into sections of the basement, or even plan on cleaning off a shelf or two at a time. Once you have sorted everything into trash, sell, give to charity, or keep, you can add list items to deal with your piles. One list item may be to throw away or haul away the trash while another could be to take bags to someone who sells things online or to charity. Then a final item may be to mop the floor. Alternatively, you can put a time amount on the note (e.g., Basement - 1 hr). This note can then be reused.

Now, from that long list of sticky notes, pick out the ones that you absolutely want to accomplish today, or tomorrow, or in the next twenty-four to thirty-six hours to comprise your "current" list. You can also choose additional notes that you will do if you have time (that is, you can have two lists, one for those tasks that you absolutely want to accomplish today and a second one for those tasks that you will work on if you have enough time). This extra list is optional. Separate the "current" list(s) from your grand list and put your grand list somewhere that you will not see it until the next day or until you finish the tasks you have in front of you.

If you tend to lose lists, place these notes on the end of a desk or table so you will always know where they are. For the grand list, choose a place where you are unlikely to see it, or cover the list with a pad of paper to hide it. Alternatively, if you use a paper planner instead of an electronic device, put your grand list in the back of your planner and put your "current" list or your "today" list in the front of the planner.

As you look at these tasks, plan an order in which you'd like to do them. Consider a few things while planning this order. First, if you have errands you want to accomplish, it might be best to take a gander at your grand list to see if there are other errands to do while you're out and about. If you have color-coded your errands this will only take a moment.

While putting your to-do items in order, consider efficiency as well as using more enjoyable list items as breaks. On the one hand, it's typically most efficient to put similar tasks together. For instance, if you have two or three tasks to accomplish outside (e.g., washing the car, weeding the garden, spreading fertilizer on the grass), it's most efficient to do all of these tasks in succession so that you don't have to clean up or go inside in between tasks. Similarly, if you want to check your e-mail, write a letter, and order something on the Web, it's quickest to do all of these while you're already at the computer, especially if you typically turn off your computer when you're not using it.

On the other hand, you may love outdoor tasks, hate housework, and find that doing computer work is somewhere in between. In such case, you might find your list to be more efficient if you use the Premack Principle. The Premack Principle states that more probable behaviors will reinforce less probable behaviors. In other words, in the aforementioned case, do the housework first, knowing that you will follow it by one of the outdoor tasks almost as a reward. The outdoor tasks can actually serve as a break from the less desirable tasks. An additional way to use the Premack Principle in your lists is to make sticky notes in your favorite color to list fun things that you do once you have completed some of your tasks (e.g., read a magazine, play a musical instrument, take a walk).

Putting the list in the order in which you want to do the tasks alleviates a lot of stress that can be caused by having to decide throughout the day what you are going to do next. It decreases the time often spent on the traditional type of list looking it over and trying to figure out what to do next. It also saves the energy you take considering what you will try to accomplish next before you even get to what's next. If you plan in advance the order in which you'd like to do things, it takes the guess work out of the day and relieves stress. For instance, I might have the following list to do for just today (I use a separate sticky for each load of laundry):

Wash Car

Laundry

Laundry

Call Mom

Grocery Store

Report

Dishes

Bookstore

Call Dentist

Weed Garden

Bank

e-mail Bob, Jill, Dan

Play Music

I can plan an order that would make sense and be efficient. For instance, if it has been really hot, I may want to accomplish the outdoor tasks first thing in the morning, or if it has been really cool I may want to wait until the afternoon. I'll want to avoid rush hour to do the errands and I'll want to think about a route for doing the errands that would make most sense (e.g., quickest routes, groceries last if it's warm). I may want to make sure there aren't other errands on my grand list. I'll want to figure out when to do the laundry that it won't sit in the dryer for too long.

Let's say it's not all that hot outside so I decide to get the first load of laundry in the washer and then run my errands. I put my list in the following order and decide to call Mom and the dentist while on my errands. I "piggy back" those tasks with my errands. When I get home I'll put the clean clothes in the dryer and the dirty ones in the washer. Then I'll do indoor tasks and enjoyable activities until my laundry is done. I'll do the outdoor tasks that I enjoy most last.

Laundry

Bank

Call Mom

Bookstore

Call Dentist

Grocery Store

Laundry

e-mail Bob, Jill, Dan

Report

Play Music

Dishes

Weed Garden

Wash Car

With efficiency in mind, place your stickies in the order in which you want to do them. Does this feel different from having made an ordinary list?

Try this exercise. Look at your grand list and your "today" list. Now look at only the "today" list. Feels better, doesn't it? Now let's take another step forward. From the "today" list, pick off one sticky note at random. Look at it and look away from the current list. Now look back at the whole list. Which feels better, looking at the one note or the list of notes? One of my favorite things about using the physical sticky notes is being able to really focus on the moment by looking at just one note at a time. After all, we really can do only one thing at a time.

The jury is no longer out. Multitasking is not typically efficient. It's best to focus on one thing at a time. On rare occasions, we might be able to handle two things at once. Otherwise you might think you're doing several things at once, but you are actually quickly alternating between tasks and not likely efficiently. Taking off just one sticky note and doing only that one task can help to bring you into the moment and release the weight of other tasks. Try to remember that regardless of whether you have one thing to do, fifty things to do, or more than a hundred things to do, you can do only one thing at a time.

Similarly, knowing that you have your tasks in order helps you to focus on the moment because you're not trying to make a decision about what to do next. For those of you who really have difficulty letting go of all of your responsibilities in favor of focusing on one task, I recommend that you go as far as putting that sticky note with the task in which you are currently engaged right in front of you (if applicable). When you go on errands, take just the errand sticky notes with you, leaving the rest behind.

For some errands you may want to have a list of things you want to buy or do for your list item. This is probably most applicable for stores. For instance, if you are going to the hardware store and that is one of your list items, you may want to make a sublist of the items you want to buy there. Other sublists may include tasks to do at the bank or questions to ask your doctor, stock broker, and so on. In these instances, you can use a larger sticky note. This may be the main advantage of using the computer and Web-based programs: the sticky can easily be enlarged depending on how much you put on it. That is, you start with a small note and it automatically expands as you put more on it. You can also print out the stickies on which you have your sublists, so you can take them with you on your errand. Finally, if you are familiar with the layout of the store you can move the items around to make your trip more efficient. This is an advantage of the computer program where it is easier to change the order of sublist items.

Sometimes you may have several things on your list that you've started, but few have been completed. When you look at what little you've accomplished it can be somewhat discouraging. Likewise, when you look at all the things that you still have not completed, it can be a bit overwhelming and may be frustrating. In such situations, showing progress can be helpful. Not all people who use sticky note lists incorporate this suggestion, but this option can help to motivate you in the aforementioned situation. My suggestion for tracking progress with your lists is to place your items in three columns with the following headings: "to do," "under way," and "completed." Alternatively, you can use the first two columns and throw away the notes once they are finished.

The point of the "under way" column is to organize those tasks that you have started, but have not yet completed, whether because of choice or temporary inability to complete them. An example of the former is that you have written a draft of a report and you feel that you work better if you let it sit and come back to it with fresh eyes later. Put the "report" sticky note in the "under way" column. An example of the latter is that you have left a message for someone. You still want to talk to the person, so you don't consider the task accomplished until you have actually spoken with her. Maybe you have a load of laundry in the washer and one in the dryer. Put each note with "laundry" on it in the "under way" column. This practice helps in two ways. First, it allows you to organize your list a little better. Second, it is a way of "getting credit" for your efforts that have yet to reach completion. If you wish to do your "under way" notes today, you can move them again to place them in the order that you'd like to do them. At the end of the day, those that are incomplete can be moved to your next day's list, making them easier to accomplish.

TO DO	UNDER WAY	DONE
Wash Car	Laundry	e-mail Bob, Jill, Dan
Weed Garden	Laundry	Grocery Store
Dishes	Call Mom	Call Dentist
	Report	Bookstore
		Bank

CELEBRATING!

With the old-fashioned list you can only scratch off or put a check or an "X" next to the list item when it's completed. With the sticky note list you can celebrate in a number of ways. You can put your note in the "done" column. You can scratch it off or put a check or "X" on the item as you have done in the past. You can crumple it up and toss it in the trash. You can also do any combination of these.

Live It!

Whether you are using sticky notes or a computer program, list your tasks individually so that you can arrange them in the order that you'd like to do them. Consider:

(1) separating your grand list from your "today" or "current" list,

(2) color coding tasks,

(3) inserting enjoyable things between tasks, and

(4) arranging tasks in such a way as to show progress on partially completed tasks.

Chapter 16

Finding Balance in an Unbalanced World

On your deathbed will you be more likely to:

a. Regret that you didn't work harder, didn't accomplish more, or didn't make more money, or

b. Regret that you didn't spend more time with loved ones and enjoying your passions?

Do you feel frustrated because your in-box (i.e., list of things to do) is usually full? Do you take great pride in those rare occasions that it's empty or even half full instead of overflowing? When it starts to get low do you find that it fills rapidly? Do you often feel the weight of your to-do list stressing you out? Moreover, do you think that you will take a break once you get everything done, but you find that this rarely, if ever, happens? If you answered "yes" to the last question then it means that work is your priority and that enjoying life is not. This may not be your intention, but it is how you are living your life; your life is clearly out of balance. If you answered "yes" to any of the other questions, you could use some help with balance and setting priorities.

When you're on your deathbed, do you think you are going to reflect back on your life and regret that you did not make more money and accomplish more? Or are you more likely to look back and think, "Gee, I spent so much time working that I didn't get much time to enjoy the people who are important to me"? Are you likely to wish that you had spent more time pursuing an interest that gives you pleasure, like traveling, hiking, or a personal hobby such as woodworking, playing music, or cooking? At the end of life there are certainly some rewards for getting a lot accomplished. But I assure you that if your number one priority is to get things accomplished, you are likely to look back and wish that you had accomplished less and enjoyed more.

With balance in mind, the previous chapter was written to help you become more efficient, thus making more time for leisure. It was also designed to help you put your to-do list out of your mind when relaxing and having fun. My hope is that you don't use the extra time to get more work accomplished. Therefore, to help you to achieve better balance I have a few things for you to think about. Start by being mindful of doing or recognizing the following:

1. *Get comfortable with your in-box never being empty and often being full.*

2. *Remember that as soon as you make it less full, you create space for more things and they are often things you don't want to do. It's easier to say "no" to creating or accepting more tasks when your in-box is full.*

3. *When there is space, rather than taking on responsibility you'd rather not have, leave that space for something you want to do.*

Most people who are reading this book probably fit into the Type A mold. If you were born after 1980 you may not remember this once popular category described as the competitive, goal-driven, high-energy type of person. Type A people tend to choose most, if not all, of their priorities as goal-directed or achievement-oriented priorities. Their in-boxes are full of things that they believe that they need to accomplish. They often base their self-worth on how much they can accomplish.

Unfortunately, this habit of doing more and more causes more negative reinforcement than positive reinforcement. In other words, rather than feeling good when you accomplish tasks, you feel relief from the weight of the tasks being over. The

Nip It in the Bud

Connect with nature. When you notice anything natural, use it as a reminder to be in the moment. Look for opportunities to connect with nature and use these sounds, sights, smells, and sensations to add an enjoyable and relaxing dimension to your life. Enjoy the sound of birds, the smell of lilacs, the sight of a beautiful sunset, and the feeling of the breeze, etc.

motivation that drives the habit of working too much is more similar to "I hit myself in the head because it feels so good when I stop" than it is to "I get to sit in a hot tub after work because it feels so good."

Negative reinforcement is very powerful. It happens when your drive and behavior increase because you are escaping or avoiding discomfort. If you feel guilty, anxious, or tense and then you cross an item off your list, you feel some level of relief. The guilt, stress, and anxiety decrease, but only temporarily. This relief reinforces that behavior. Instead of feeling proud of your accomplishments and rewarding yourself with something enjoyable, you get negatively reinforced for crossing the item off your list, and this motivates you to put something else on your list so that you feel that relief again. When you feel this negative reinforcement, you tend to repeat the pattern over and over again by continuing to add more things to your list. Getting tasks accomplished can be positively reinforcing too, but the danger is in falling out of balance. When you are more motivated by negative reinforcement than by positive reinforcement, or when you are finding less and less time to do things you'd rather be doing, balance is lost and you wind up unhappy.

I'm not saying that your in-box is necessarily full of things you don't like doing. In fact, I hope that you get pleasure out of your work and feel a positive sense of pride and accomplishment when you complete some things. What I'm talking about is the feeling that you can't relax until you finish everything and only feel good after you accomplish stuff.

The costs of the stress and what you miss in life outweigh the positives of accomplishment. In addition, the more you try to accomplish for the sake of getting it crossed off your list and "getting it done," the less you are likely to enjoy it. There are as many as three reasons for this. One reason is that you can become so focused on getting it done that you forget about what you may have once enjoyed and why it can be enjoyable. That is, gratification is lost because the focus is on getting it "crossed off your list" and the very temporary relief of completing the task. A second reason is that you are focused on the future. You focus on getting it finished, and often on what you're going to do next, instead of being in the moment. The third reason is negative reinforcement as explained earlier.

Now that's not to say that you shouldn't sometimes feel proud of your creative projects being finished. It can also be great to have a positive work ethic. And yes, many good things can come from having that strong work ethic. For example, you can afford to buy that hot tub that feels so good. But what use is the hot tub if you don't use it? What good is that beautiful home if you rarely enjoy it because you are usually working? To what extent are the costs not worth the benefits? The bottom line is that it is about balance. It's about learning to be very efficient when you work and often making leisurely activities a priority so that you can find time to relax or have fun. Another way to think of it is that a great work ethic is useless if you don't enjoy the fruits of your labor. Rather than becoming more efficient so that you can get more work accomplished, I challenge you to break the cycle of negative reinforcement and work more efficiently so that you have more time to relax and play.

The best way to break that cycle of negative reinforcement is to do fun and relaxing things despite the guilt and anxiety, because eventually those uncomfortable feelings will likely subside. In addition, take a break from your lists on a regular basis. Lists can be very helpful, but if you rely on them too much they can contribute to your stress.

Another way to help find balance is to stop making all of your priorities work-related. We have work schedules; we schedule appointments with doctors; we schedule time with friends and relatives; but how often do we schedule time for ourselves?

Instead of waiting until your in-box is empty or low to take time for yourself, think about what you really want to do that you haven't been doing. Whether it's starting to read the novel you bought three months ago, trying that new recipe, shooting pool, or playing music, schedule it. Take a look at your schedule right now and look for a time that you can make this fun or relaxing thing

> ### B³s and Balance
>
> Some people have a difficult time wrapping their heads around taking free time to enjoy life. If you find that you are concerned that you are wasting time, that you don't deserve to have balance in your life, or have some other unhelpful belief that prevents you from being more balanced, you may want to develop a B³ mantra. For example: I want to enjoy my life more and I deserve it. The things that I work so hard for are only worth having if I take time to enjoy them. We work so we can play.

a priority and leave your to-do list behind. Consider it to be an appointment with yourself. Don't reschedule it if something comes up unless it's a true emergency.

A similar alternative is to carve out "me time" the same time each day. Maybe you will decide not to work (including household chores) after 9:00 p.m. for instance. Or perhaps you'll extend your lunch hour by thirty minutes to do something you enjoy. Just make sure you protect that time with very few exceptions.

When carving out time for fun you may feel guilty at first because the negative reinforcement has increased your guilt. Don't give in to the guilt. The more you prioritize fun things and refrain from giving in to guilt, the more your guilt will decline. Over time the old habit of negatively reinforcing your guilt will be replaced with the positive reinforcement of enjoying yourself.

In addition to finding more time for fun and relaxation, I encourage you to tap into the intrinsic sense of enjoyment, motivation, and challenge in your work. Often when we put things on our to-do lists they become chores and our mind-set is to get them crossed off our lists rather than finding the intrinsic enjoyment in at least some of the tasks. This can include our regular job schedules. As stated in Chapter 9, we often think of items on our schedules as "need to's" or "shoulds" even when they are things we want to do.

In the film *Jerry Maguire*, Tom Cruise played the title role as a sports agent who was representing Rod Tidwell, an NFL football star played by Cuba Gooding, Jr. Rod was upset that he didn't get as much money as other football stars and felt he deserved more. He continually pestered Jerry about trying to get him more money and regardless of what Jerry said, he repeatedly replied: "Show me the MONEY" with big, dramatic displays of frustration. Midway through the film Jerry asked him if he started playing football for money. Rod said "no." Jerry then asked him why he started playing and why he kept playing those first few years. Rod started to talk passionately about the game, as opposed to the money, for the first time in the film. He realized that football had been really fun and at least some viewers got the sense that his focus on the money had been robbing him of the joy of playing. As a result of their conversation, Rod started to have more fun and ended up getting more money too. Often, when you follow the intrinsic motivation, the extrinsic will come. Rod Tidwell was an example of that as after he started playing more for his passion, he got the money.

Another example is from an episode of *Northern Exposure*, a TV show that aired in the 1990s. The episode opened with a man named Holling smiling while painting, with upbeat music playing. He finished his work and then showed it to his friends, who liked it so much that they put in orders for him to paint for them. Holling agreed, but he quickly lost the enjoyment of painting. He decided to speak with Chris, a very spiritual character whose advice people often sought. Chris told Holling that he was confusing process with product. He explained that he had enjoyed the painting while focusing on painting, but once he focused on finishing the product for other people or for money, he no longer enjoyed it. Holling was still confused, so Chris had him bring in his first painting, which he promptly threw it into the incinerator. He then said something like, "You lost your product, but you didn't lose the enjoyment of the process of painting."

I can find examples in my own life as well. In my first semester of grad school I kept trying to get "A's," and when I studied I was focused on memorizing to get the grades. I was miserable. Early in my second semester, two things happened to help me become more balanced. First my roommate pointed out that all of my priorities were work and that I kept saying I'd play when my work was finished, but I rarely played because I almost always had work that could be done. This led me to speak to my department chair, who assured me that I could get all "B's" and it wouldn't affect my career at all. The culmination was a paradigm shift. I realized that I was passionate about becoming a great psychologist. Therefore, instead of studying to get "A's," I studied what I thought I'd want to know to accomplish that goal. I also began to carve out time twice a week to have fun and twice per week to exercise. I ended up with straight "A's" that semester, after getting a "B" in my less balanced semester. Moreover, I was much happier.

Today, I look forward to moments like the one I had with Jane, when her tears and panic turned to relief and a huge smile in seconds. I enjoy the bittersweet days when I say "goodbye" to a client because he is feeling relaxed and balanced. It's very gratifying when someone comes in and explains how something I had said in the previous appointment really "clicked" and made a positive impact in their life.

Think about why you chose your field of work. What is it that initially inspired you? Make sure to connect with the intrinsic motivation, that is, the motivation of enjoyment or satisfaction. I really believe that if you follow your intrinsic motivation, rather than the extrinsic motivation, you will be duly rewarded for it. Not only will you enjoy your work more, but because you enjoy it more you will be more motivated, more creative, and have more energy left at the end of the day and at the beginning of the next. Therefore, the extrinsic reward will be greater.

In author Pam Houston's memoir *A Little More About Me*, she explains how the meaning of success has changed for her. In a chapter titled "Redefining Success," she writes:

> ...[M]y first notion of success, came from my parents and involved country clubs, clothing, and cars. As I became an adult I replaced that list with a list of my own, no less arbitrary: a Ph.D., a book of short stories, a place on a best-seller list, a film. But now I am coming to the understanding that success has less to do with the accumulation of things and more to do with an accumulation of moments, and that creating a successful life might be as simple as determining which moments are the most valuable, and seeing how many of those I can string together in a line.

I was thinking about this recently as I rode my bike through Forest Park, one of the largest city parks in the country, enjoying the sunshine and the blue sky, painted with a few white and gray puffy clouds. I felt the wind on my face and arms as I moved forward on my bike soaking up the changing landscape, with flowers, ponds, birds and a variety of architecture. I reveled in the beauty while challenging myself to a longer than usual ride. Despite how much I enjoyed the longer ride, I also took pleasure in the relief that I could rest and was gratified by a pleasurable sense of accomplishment. I reflected on my ride as I shared wine, food, conversation, and laughs with friends outdoors at a small café and as I drove home with the top down enjoying the comfortable breeze.

Mastercard has capitalized on this idea for years, with their "priceless" campaign, which taps into the moments to which Pam Houston and I refer. Take a few moments to reflect upon the priceless moments in your life. How many of them involved a traditional example of success? How many of them involved friends, loved ones, or a personal sense of enjoyment that money can't buy?

Try out this new perspective on success for yourself. To bring balance to your life, define success as the number and intensity of quality moments such as connecting with nature or people, laughing, learning something really interesting, experiencing a birth, creating art, playing music, and even weathering and overcoming obstacles. Look for these moments; create these moments; enjoy them.

Embracing these moments interwoven into your life will play a big part in creating balance and happiness. Along with the other tools in this book, I believe you can achieve a state of active relaxation while you negotiate through all the challenges that life brings. I wish you the best in effectively implementing the active relaxation strategies to help you achieve a new definition of success in your life.

Live It!

1. Think about how your life would be different if you worked 10 percent, 25 percent, or 50 percent less. Consider changes in your life that will allow you to have 10 to 50 percent more free time. This may be by reducing your hours or workload directly, hiring someone to do some of your work, or improving your efficiency.

2. Think about what you do with your free time and consider what you would rather do with that time. Make a plan to improve your success as defined by the frequency and quality of enjoyable moments. Include scheduling time to make this a priority.

3. Reconnect with the intrinsic joy you get from the process of doing your work.

References for Active Relaxation

Beck, A.T. 1975. *Cognitive Therapy and the Emotional Disorders.* Madison, Conn.: International Universities Press

Bernstein, D., and Borkovec T.D. 1973. *Progressive Relaxation Training: A Manual for the Helping Professions.* Champaign, Ill.: Research Press.

Borkovec, T. D. and E. Costello, 1993. "Efficacy of Applied Relaxation and Cognitive-Behavioral in the Treatment of Generalized Anxiety Disorder." *Journal of Consulting and Clinical Psychology.*
61(4) : 611-619.

Burns, D. D. 1980. *Feeling Good: The New Mood Therapy.* New York, NY. Wm. Morrow and Co.

Dugas, M. J., Letarte, H., Rhéaume, J., Freeston, M. and Ladouceur R.1995. "Worry and Problem Solving: Evidence of a Specific Relationship." *Cognitive Therapy and Research.* 19(1) : 109-120.

Ellis, A. 1975. *A New Guide to Rational Living.* Upper Saddle River, N.J.: Prentice-Hall.

Epstein, M. 1998. *Going to Pieces Without Falling Apart: A Buddhist's Perspective on Wholeness.* New York, NY: Broadway Books.

Hazlette-Stevens, H. 2005. *Women Who Worry Too Much: How to Stop Worry & Anxiety from Ruining Relationships, Work, & Fun.* Oakland, Calif.: New Harbinger.

Herz, R. 2007. *The Scent of Desire: Discovering Our Enigmatic Sense of Smell.* New York, NY.: HarperCollins

Houston, P. 2000. *A Little More About Me.* New York, N.Y.: Washington Square Press.

Jacobsen, E. 1938. *Progressive Relaxation.* Chicago: University of Chicago Press.

Jakubowski, P. and Lange, A.J. 1978. *The Assertive Option: Your Rights and Responsibilities.* Champaign, IL: Research Press

Kabat-Zinn, J. 1990. *Full Catastrophe Living: Using the Wisdom of Your Body and Mind to Face Stress, Pain, and Illness.* New York: New York, Random House, Inc.

Ristad, E. 1981. *A Soprano on Her Head: Right-Side-Up Reflections on Life and Other Performances.* London: Dorian Press.

Warner Bros. Pictures. 2001. *Harry Potter and the Sorcerer's Stone.*

Wegner, D. 1989. *White Bears and Other Unwanted Thoughts.* New York: Guilford Press.

Dr. Jennifer L. Abel is available for corporate consulting and a variety of workshops. You may contact her on her website: www.anxietystlouispsychologist.com

CPSIA information can be obtained
at www.ICGtesting.com
Printed in the USA
FFOW01n1708090514
5244FF